STORMING
THE GATES OF
HEAVEN

STORMING THE GATES OF HEAVEN

THE PRAYER THAT CLAIMS
THE PROMISES OF GOD

ANNE
GRAHAM
LOTZ

CONTENTS

IT'S TIME TO STORM THE GATES OF HEAVEN

The atmosphere was thick with the presence of God.

We were in Suva, Fiji, where Samaritan's Purse was hosting a conference for church workers. Six hundred people had come in from the dozens of surrounding islands to attend. I had just finished speaking on the prophet Samuel, presenting the tragic truth that while he was a judge, a prophet, and a kingmaker extraordinaire, Samuel was not a good father. His sons did not follow the Lord. My challenge to the mostly male audience was not to be so focused on ministry that they neglected their own family.

When I issued the invitation to commit to training

up their children in the Lord, almost the entire audience of pastors and church leaders surged forward. They began pouring out their hearts, urgently pleading with God to forgive, to have mercy, to bless.

I remember a woman seizing me by the arm and pulling me into her circle for prayer. *Pray?* I was totally intimidated to pray in such a group. When I opened my mouth and tried, my voice sounded hollow. My prayer seemed wretchedly anemic in the midst of such fervent intensity.

Rarely have I ever heard prayer like I heard on that day in Suva, Fiji. This has led me to wonder why our prayers often lack that kind of power, passion, and persuasion. What are we missing? What was *I missing?*

Could it be that one missing ingredient is a no-holds-barred, go-for-broke, nothing-held-back commitment to pray? The kind of commitment that's born out of desperation. Intense aspiration. Soulful longing. The kind of commitment athletes make to win the race, the game, the trophy, the medal.

The prayer that storms the gates of Heaven—the kind that Daniel prayed—is not a run-of-the-mill, garden-variety type of prayer. It's a commitment that perseveres over any and every obstacle until God's promises have been claimed and His purposes fulfilled.

Daniel's original prayer was a desperate plea uttered by one man on behalf of his nation, Judah, that had come under God's judgment. When the ten northern tribes of Israel had embraced idolatry—refusing to heed God's repeated warnings of judgment if there was no national repentance of sin—God had sent in the Assyrians, who destroyed the Northern Kingdom.[1] The Southern Kingdom of Judah, with the smaller tribe of Benjamin, was the remaining remnant of what had been the nation of Israel under King David and his successor-son, Solomon.

Now God was issuing those same warnings to Judah. He had sent messenger after messenger, including the prophets Jeremiah, Habakkuk, and Zephaniah, who had each faithfully delivered the message with every conceivable emphasis and nuance. They spoke clearly, powerfully, emotionally, factually, and accurately. The people were left with no excuse for not "getting it." But the nation of Judah refused to heed God's warnings, and so judgment fell.

Judgment came in the form of the Babylonians, who were ruled by the ruthless emperor Nebuchadnezzar. Following their conquest of two major world powers—Assyria, then Egypt—they swept through Judah, leveled Jerusalem, looted the temple treasures, and forcibly took God's people to Babylon in a series of three deportations, effectively enslaving the entire population. In a relatively short period of time, Judah was erased from the national scene. After more than five hundred years of existence, she was a people and a nation in exile.

Daniel was approximately fifteen years of age when he was captured by the Babylonians and deported eight hundred miles east of Jerusalem to serve as a slave in Nebuchadnezzar's court. His situation seemed utterly hopeless and helpless. He had no human rights commission to appeal to, no dream team of lawyers to represent him. He was abducted to serve an emperor who had absolute world power and was accountable to no one. Yet through it all, Daniel glorified God by his character and his conduct. His service was so extraordinary that he rapidly rose up through the ranks to become a national leader as well as a counselor to kings.

As young as he was, Daniel may not have known about the power of prayer from experience. But as his story unfolds, it's clear he knew something about the power of his God, perhaps based on his nation's history. And it didn't take long for Daniel to discover the power of God through prayer. Again and again he threw himself upon God with such complete faith that God came through for him. Powerfully. Personally. Dramatically. Repeatedly.

Daniel's meteoric rise to prominence is remarkable because, despite being subjected to a kind of cultural brainwashing upon arriving in Babylon, he again and again maintained his undivided devotion to God. In turn, Daniel rose to be the equivalent of prime minister under four emperors. And yet Daniel never forgot the temple that had been the heart of Jerusalem and of the nation. Even at the end of his life, he remained mindful of the sacrifices that had been offered to God there in worship. He longed for Jerusalem every day of his life, evidenced by the fact that three times daily, when he prayed, he turned his face in the direction of his beloved city that once had been.

Again and again, Daniel's life was threatened. But each time, in response to his remarkable, steadfast faith, God miraculously intervened, until He performed the greatest miracle of all in answer to Daniel's prayer: moving Emperor Cyrus to issue the decree that after seventy years of captivity, every Jew living in Babylon could go home.

What kind of prayer was it that, when offered by one person on behalf of a people who were under God's judgment, moved Heaven and changed a nation?[2] What can we learn today from Daniel's prayer that would similarly move Heaven and change our beloved nation? Even after a full generation of apostasy and separation from national faith in the living God, is it possible that the prayer of one person could bring renewal, restoration, and revival to America?

That's what I want to find out.

I believe it's time to pray like Daniel.

Now.

For nothing, *nothing*—no politics or president, no government or agreement, no institution or organization, no media or ministry, no economy or military, no alliance or treaty—will turn our nation around except heartfelt, desperate prayer. Prayer where the pray-ers rend their hearts, return to the Cross, and repent of personal and national sin.

Only prayer that storms the gates of Heaven with the promises of God can change a nation. Only prayer like Daniel's.

DANIEL'S ORIGINAL PRAYER

DANIEL 9:1–23

In the first year of Darius . . . , who was made ruler over the Babylonian kingdom— . . . I, Daniel, understood from the Scriptures, according to the word of the Lord given to Jeremiah the prophet, that the desolation of Jerusalem would last seventy years. So I turned to the Lord God and pleaded with him in prayer and petition, in fasting, and in sackcloth and ashes.

I prayed to the LORD my God and confessed:

"O Lord, the great and awesome God, who keeps his covenant of love with all who love him and obey his commands, we have sinned and done wrong. We have been wicked and have rebelled; we have turned away from your commands and laws. We have not listened to your servants the prophets, who spoke in your name to our kings, our princes and our fathers, and to all the people of the land.

"Lord, you are righteous, but this day we are covered with shame—the men of Judah and the people of Jerusalem and all Israel, both near and far, in all the countries where you have scattered us because of our unfaithfulness to you. O Lord, we and our kings, our princes and our ancestors are covered with shame because we have sinned against you. The Lord our God is merciful and forgiving, even though we have rebelled against him; we have not obeyed the Lord our God or kept the laws he gave us through his servants the prophets. All Israel has transgressed your law and turned away, refusing to obey you.

"Therefore the curses and sworn judgments written in the Law of Moses, the servant of God, have been poured out on us, because we have sinned against you. You have fulfilled the words spoken against us and against our rulers by bringing on us great disaster. Under the whole heaven nothing has ever been done like what has been done to Jerusalem. Just as it is written in the Law of Moses, all this disaster has come upon us, yet we have not sought the favor of the Lord our God by turning from our sins and giving attention to your truth. The LORD did not hesitate to bring the disaster upon us, for the LORD our God is righteous in everything he does; yet we have not obeyed him.

"Now, O Lord our God, who brought your people out of Egypt with a mighty hand and who made for yourself a name that endures to this day, we have sinned, we have done wrong. O Lord, in keeping with all your righteous acts, turn away your anger and your wrath from Jerusalem, your city, your holy hill. Our sins and the iniquities of our fathers have made Jerusalem and your people an object of scorn to all those around us.

"Now, our God, hear the prayers and petitions of your servant. For your sake, O Lord, look with favor on your desolate sanctuary. Give ear, O God, and hear; open your eyes and see the desolation of the city that bears your Name. We do not make requests of you because we are righteous, but because of your great mercy. O Lord, listen! O Lord, forgive! O Lord, hear and act! For your sake, O my God, do not delay, because your city and your people bear your Name."

While I was speaking and praying, confessing my sin and the sin of my people Israel and making my request to the LORD my God for his holy hill—while I was still in prayer, Gabriel, the man I had seen in the earlier vision, came to me in swift flight about the time of the evening sacrifice. He instructed me and said to me, "Daniel, I have now come to give you insight and understanding. As soon as you began to pray, an answer was given, which I have come to tell you, for you are highly esteemed."

PART 1

PREPARING
FOR PRAYER

Devote yourselves to prayer,
being watchful and thankful.
COLOSSIANS 4:2

CHAPTER 1

COMMITTED
TO PRAY

It is said that Susanna Wesley, mother to nine-teen children including John and Charles, used to throw her apron up over her face to have a few private moments for her prayers. I once heard a Bible teacher share that when her three children were small, she let them run loose in the house; then she would climb into their playpen to grab a few moments of private prayer. My own mother encouraged me to "pray on the hoof"—wherever I was and in whatever I was doing.

It was her paraphrase of what the apostle Paul told the Thessalonian Christians when he instructed them to "pray without ceasing."[1]

While I am well aware that we can pray anytime, anywhere, about anything, Daniel's prayer is different. It's a commitment. And I am convinced our commitments, or lack of them, change our lives.

The most important commitment I ever made has been to be a disciple of Jesus Christ. It determines the way I spend my money and my time, the friends I have and the enemies I make, the habits I establish and the habits I break, where I go and what I do. It's a commitment that has been life-altering and life-shaping.

I made another life-altering, life-shaping commitment when I said yes to the marriage proposal offered by Danny Lotz. It led me to a milestone moment on September 2, 1966, at 8:00 in the evening. I stood in the double doorway of Gaither Chapel in Montreat, North Carolina, the small Presbyterian church in which I had been raised. My hand was looped through Daddy's arm as we waited for the wedding director to signal that it was time to walk down the aisle. The stone chapel was packed with hundreds of special friends and guests as Daddy and I proceeded to walk on the same aisle cloth that he and my mother had walked twenty-three years earlier, when they had been married.

We met my eager bridegroom, grinning from ear to ear, at the front of the chapel. My father kissed my cheek, placed my hand in Danny's, then stepped in front of us and led us through our wedding vows, pronouncing us man and wife. When I said, "I do," I knew there was no turning back. Because marriage is a commitment.

That commitment required time. Energy. Sacrifice. It affected me in every way, at every level, on every day. It wasn't easy, but God blessed our relationship. It was challenging at times to maintain, especially when I became Danny's full-time caregiver. But I made the commitment to be his wife. And I followed through on that commitment until Jesus took Danny home.[2]

The duration and depth of my marriage commitment help me to understand the divine dynamic of love and sacrifice that are requirements if we are to experience God's faithfulness throughout life's mountains and valleys. And that's Daniel's prayer. It's a commitment to storm the gates of Heaven until the prayer is answered, motivated by a wholehearted love that's willing to suffer, to repent, to do whatever it takes to get an answer.

By his own example, one of the things Daniel teaches us is that his commitment to pray required preparation. Just as an athlete can't expect to win by showing up at game time without having practiced, the commitment to pray doesn't just happen.

A Prepared Place for Prayer

Daniel had a specific place designated for prayer: an upstairs room in his home to which he withdrew three times every day.[3]

His preparations may have been as simple as setting aside this particular place where he could be undistracted and undisturbed. I'm convinced we all need this kind of sacred space for time alone with God.

My prepared place for prayer is the corner of my living room. On one side of the chair where I sit is a fireplace in which I light a fire on cold winter mornings. On the other side is a table with a drawer in which I keep several translations of the Bible, three small devotional books, a Bible-study notebook, a personal journal, my reading glasses, pencil, pen, legal pad, iPad, and tissues. I want everything in place so that once I sit down to pray, I don't have to keep jumping up to find what I need.

I have also set aside a place for prayer in my ministry office. I did this when, in my early-morning devotional study of Exodus, I was struck by the fact that Moses had set aside a tent outside the camp of Israel and designated it for prayer. I selected a room in the center of the building and placed enough chairs in it for every staff person who serves at AnGeL Ministries. I had the walls painted a navy blue to give it a quiet, secluded atmosphere. At one end of the room is a small bench in front of a large cross. At the other end of the room is an easy chair with a table beside it on which is a lamp, a box of tissues, a Bible, and a card box containing prayer requests people send to our ministry. Outside I hung a small framed sign: The Meeting Place.[4]

While God meets us wherever and whenever we call out to him, a Daniel-like commitment requires preparation in order to maximize the impact of our prayers. Do you have a designated Meeting Place? Would you consider establishing one? Make the commitment to place prayer at the heart of your home or office.

I understand that not everyone has the space to set aside. When my sister's children were young and she was living in a small house, she kept her Bible-study materials in a cardboard box underneath her sofa in the family room. When she had a few moments, she pulled out her box and had everything she needed for prayer. She found a way to make it work within the context of her circumstances—something we all can do.

A Prepared Time for Prayer

I know business professionals who go to their office an hour earlier in the morning to have time for prayer. Their "materials" have been downloaded on electronic devices.[5] Would you not only consider designating a place in your home or office for prayer, but would you make the commitment to do so?

Prayer helps us anchor our faith in God. It's like setting our spiritual compass so that, regardless of the twists and turns during the day, the needle of our focused faith always turns to God.

Daniel's life was anchored in prayer. He established the habit of meeting God in his designated place for prayer three times a day, and he maintained that commitment even in the face of life-threatening attack.[6] Do you have a set-aside time to meet with God? When do you pray?

For years, I battled getting up early in the morning for prayer. I knew that any time during the day is acceptable to God, but I couldn't seem to shake the conviction that early-morning hours were the ideal time. The woman who taught me how to study and teach the Bible, Miss A. Wetherell Johnson, said that when our prayer time is at night, it's like tuning our violin when the symphony is over. While it's wonderful to end our day in prayer, she urged me to pray in the morning when the day before me is a blank page yet to be lived out.

I was also aware that a morning time of prayer is frequently referred to in the Bible. Just in the Psalms alone there are repeated references:

> "In the morning, O Lord, you hear my voice;
> in the morning I lay my requests before you
> and wait in expectation."

"I cry to you for help, O LORD; in the morning my prayer comes before you."

"Let the morning bring me word of your unfailing love, for I have put my trust in you. Show me the way I should go, for to you I lift up my soul."[7]

While these examples encouraged me, the one that drew me to make a commitment to an early-morning time with the Lord was the example of Jesus Himself. Mark reveals that after a pressure-packed day of intense ministry, "very early in the morning, while it was still dark, Jesus got up, left the house and went off to a solitary place, where he prayed."[8]

I felt God was directing me to establish a prayer time in the morning. But I'm not a morning person. So although I felt convicted of disobedience when I slept to the last minute, I made no real decision to get up early and pray. There were actually times when I slept in and complained to God that He hadn't awakened me for my prayer time! Or I would wake up, but then would deliberately roll over mumbling, "God, yesterday was frantically busy, and I got to bed so late last night. I'm just too tired today. I know You understand."

Yes, He did understand, but He also understood that I had never really made the commitment. I had good intentions but not obedient actions.

And then God spoke to me very firmly and clearly. I was studying and meditating on His letters to the seven churches in Revelation in order to teach them to others. Let me paraphrase His words that lovingly scalded and scolded:

Anne, I hold you in one hand and the Holy Spirit in the other hand, like balance scales. I've weighed your life against His, and you don't measure up. I know what you've been doing. You are in ministry, traveling around the world, telling other people about Me and getting them to listen to My voice, but you are not listening to Me yourself. You have a reputation of being alive—people regard you as an exemplary Christian—but from My perspective you are falling short, spiritually dying on the inside. The prayers of your prayer team are not a substitute for your own prayers. Wake up! . . . I have not found your deeds complete in My sight because you are prayerless. Remember, therefore, what I have told you and repent.[9]

Talk about a wake-up call! I went down to the gadget store at the local mall, bought a clock that sounded like a seven-fire alarm when it went off, and set it for thirty minutes ahead of when I usually got up to start my day. The first morning it went off, it scared me silly. My heart was thumping out of my chest, my poor husband was startled out of his wits and yelled, "What in the world is that?" and I knew there was no chance I was going to roll over and go back to sleep.

At last I had achieved victory over those blankets in the morning! But when I calmed down, I was still sleepy as I went to pray. Therefore I knew I had to make even more preparation for my early-morning prayer time.

This is what I came up with. After bounding out of bed in the morning the moment the alarm went off, after doing my stretches on the floor to loud worship music, after walking-jogging outside for two-and-a-half miles, after getting a triple shot of espresso in my latte at the coffee house, *then* I would come back wide awake for my prayer time.

And that worked!

It still works for me today, although I no longer need an alarm to get me up. Getting up for early-morning prayer has become one of the joys of my life. And thirty minutes is no longer close to being sufficient, although there are days when my obligations don't allow me to carve out any more time. When my schedule remains open, my daily time with the Lord can stretch into hours. I love it! I can't wait to meet the Lord in my designated place at the designated time. But it took a firm decision, practical preparations, and dedicated follow-through to get me to this point. Storming the gates of heaven requires acting on your commitment.

There is one other aspect to my preparation that I

quickly learned the hard way. It's quite obvious but not always as easy to practice. If I am to get up earlier in the morning, I *must*—this is not optional—go to bed earlier the night before. So I do.

While every aspect of our prayer doesn't necessarily need to be uttered in one place at one time, I believe the Daniel Prayer requires a set-aside place at a dedicated time to truly be effective. You can decide the place and time that are most helpful to you for focusing on prayer. The important thing is that you follow through with a consistent commitment.

A Prepared Attitude for Prayer

Daniel's body language helped him remember as he prayed that he, a slave in exile, had an audience with the One who is the living God, All Glorious, Most Holy, the Ancient of Days, the Almighty. The One who would never forsake His people.[10] When Daniel bowed his knees to God, it was a gesture of his reverence, submission, and allegiance to the One so much greater than himself or any world ruler.

Have you ever prayed on your knees? Try it. The difference your outward position makes in your inner attitude as you pray may surprise you.

Daniel not only prayed from a kneeling position, but

he made a habit of giving thanks to God. He cultivated an "attitude of gratitude" despite circumstances that were less than ideal. Think about it. His enemies were lurking outside his window, plotting his death. He was over eighty years old and still enslaved eight hundred miles from home. He served a ruthless king who had destroyed his beloved city and butchered countless people, many of whom I'm sure Daniel had known and loved. His boyhood dreams of ever seeing his beloved Jerusalem again had faded. And *still* he was thankful.

What about you? Are you thankful . . .

when your expectations, goals, and dreams have not been realized?

when your life's circumstances go from bad to worse?

when your critics are watching every move you make, anxious to catch you in something they can use to discredit you?

when you are enslaved by a body of pain, an abusive spouse, a demanding employer, or an uncaring parent?

How can anyone be thankful in those circumstances?

Daniel's attitude illustrates one of the great secrets of trusting God. The key to thankfulness is not to view God through the lens of our circumstances, but to view our circumstances through the lens of God's love and sovereign purpose. Daniel knew, as he entered his winter years, that despite the lack of comfort and ease in his life, all things had worked together for his good to enable him to fulfill God's purpose.[11] As a result, Daniel lived a life of greatness. Perhaps from Heaven's perspective, there is no greater prophet in the Old Testament than Daniel. We are still referring to his prophecies to make sense of what we see happening in our world today.

Daniel's faithfulness to God also distinguished him from among those around him. With God's favor, he rose quickly through the Babylonian system. During his lifetime, he served as a counselor to the king, as a provincial governor, then as prime minister. And his knowledge of astronomy is acknowledged as having influenced the wise men who, approximately five hundred years later, traveled from the east to worship the newborn King of the Jews in Bethlehem.[12]

Simply put, Daniel was remarkable.

If he had given in to self-pity, anger, resentment, bitterness, unforgiveness, or a vengeful spirit with a "Why me?" attitude toward God, I doubt we would ever have heard of him. Instead, three times a day, every day, Daniel found reasons to be thankful.

What is your attitude? Especially when you're in "captivity"—barred in some way from what you want to do, where you want to go, who you want to be, or what you want to have. When God has allowed you to be in some sort of exile—cut off from friends, family, that which is familiar; when He has denied you personal prosperity or happiness—are you thankful to Him?

Don't settle for less than fulfilling completely the potential that God had in mind for you when He brought you into existence, then brought you to Himself in a personal relationship. Yield your life to God's purpose even when it may seem the very opposite of anything you thought you wanted. While God's purpose may be radically different than the one you had laid out, make no mistake about it, His plan is much greater and broader . . . more lasting and impactful . . . than any plan you could come up with for yourself. I know from personal experience. And so did Daniel.

CHAPTER 2

COMPELLED
TO PRAY

I loved growing up in the Montreat Presbyterian Church. It's where I was baptized, where I gave my first public testimony, and where I was married. One of my earliest memories in church was of Dr. Fogarty, who pastored there when I was a little girl. I'm not sure if he was old at the time or just seemed old to me because I was a child, but he made a vivid impression. He wore a long, black flowing robe that billowed out behind him when he walked. But his pastoral prayers are what stand out most.

With all due respect, he prayed forever! When he bowed his head to pray, I would put my head on my grandmother's soft shoulder and drift off. It was easy to fall asleep when Dr. Fogarty prayed because his fluid voice was so sing-songy.

Recalling those childhood memories, I now wonder what my prayers sound like to others. We Christians learn to pray in certain ways because that's what good Christian people do, right? We pray for our children. Our friends. Our church. Our nation. We pray that God would bless the missionaries and all the children in Africa. And we feel pretty good about ourselves for doing it, especially if we can do so without stuttering.

Daniel's prayer is dramatically different. Instead of socially conditioned small talk, his prayer storms the gates of Heaven with what Eugene Peterson calls "reversed thunder"—praying God's Word back to Him. It's prayer that penetrates Heaven and reaps God's promises. There is nothing formulaic about it. It is laser-focused, soul-gripping, I-won't-let-You-go-until-You-bless-me kind of prayer.

When was the last time you heard someone pray like that, to the point that you became more aware of the One to whom the person was speaking than you were of the person doing the speaking? When was the last time *you* prayed like that? *Is there a secret to that kind of praying?*

The answers lie in Daniel's prayer. A prayer prayed

under compulsion. A prayer born deep within the soul that erupts up through the heart and pours out on the lips in an unselfconscious flow of words infused with the Spirit of God.

COMPELLED BY PROBLEMS IN OUR WORLD

Daniel's prayer pulsates with this type of emotional conviction. His life for sixty-seven years had been difficult at best. As an old man, he lived through another violent regime change as the Medo-Persian Empire overthrew the Babylonians. His position was uncertain under the new ruler. He may have felt an increasing apprehension about the security of his people's future. At the very least, he was living in an unsettled, rapidly changing world, implied by the brief statement, "In the first year of Darius . . . , who was made ruler over the Babylonian kingdom . . ." (9:1).[1] But rather than wring his hands, Daniel opened up his copy of the Scriptures to see what God had to say. In the end, it was the combination of the problems in his world and the promises in God's Word that ignited a fire in his heart, compelling him to give voice to his prayer.

Daniel's prayer is one birthed under pressure, squeezing the coal of our heartache, grief, and desperation into the diamond of genuine faith that pleases

God and moves Heaven. It's a plea for something you intensely long for that you know will take place, but has not taken place yet.

To be honest, I am not gripped by that kind of intensity and compulsion every time I pray. Sometimes, however, there has been no other way I could pray.

When I struggled with infertility, longed to get pregnant, but month after month, did not . . .

When I was confined to a small home with small children and yet deeply desired to serve the Lord in full-time ministry . . .

When the door of service was opened and I found myself in the pulpit looking at five hundred upturned, expectant faces waiting to hear what I was going to say . . .

When I have stood on the platform in a prison auditorium in North Carolina, the General Assembly of the United Nations, the funeral services for each of my parents, and many, many other places where I felt way in over my head . . .

When I sat in the hospital chapel with the family of my close friend who was being taken off of life support after a sudden virus . . .

When I overheard my son and his first wife in a heated argument that signaled the beginning of the end of their marriage . . .

When I returned home with my children after
having been gone for two hours and found
everything of value in the house taken by
thieves . . .

When I discovered my seventy-eight-year-old
husband in our pool, unresponsive . . .

On occasions like these, simple, memorized, mechan-
ical, now-I-lay-me-down-to-sleep types of prayer just
won't do. The prayer that storms the gates of Heaven
is an outpouring of heartfelt emotion and passionate
pleading based on God's Word as we hold Him to His
promises.

COMPELLED BY THE
PROMISES IN GOD'S WORD

In each of the situations above, God had given me a
promise, and it was His promise that was the basis for
my prayer . . .

When I longed to get pregnant, but month after
month did not, God promised me in 1 Samuel 1:17 that
He would grant what I had asked of Him. In time, I
not only gave birth to a son, but to two daughters.

When I was confined to a small home with small
children and deeply desired to serve the Lord, He
revealed from Hosea 2:14 that He had intentionally

placed me in the "wilderness" so that I would learn to listen to His voice. His Word was true. I did not waste my wilderness years, but studied the Scriptures, and thus was prepared when He called me out to teach the Bible to others.

When the door of service was opened and I found myself in the pulpit looking at five hundred expectant faces, He clearly confirmed my call in Jeremiah 1:4–7 to go wherever He sent me and to say whatever He commanded me. Although my timidity and shyness caused me to be physically sick before I spoke for the first six weeks of teaching, I remembered His word that I was "not to be afraid of their faces" and so did not give in to the fear.

When I have stood in many, many places where I was in over my head, He assured me from John 3:34 that He would give me His Spirit without limit. I have now experienced His promised sufficiency for more than forty years as He has faithfully equipped, enabled, and empowered me to be fully obedient to His call.

When I sat in the hospital chapel with the family of my dear friend who was being taken off of life support, the Lord conveyed to me His anger over the temporary victory death seemed to have, but immediately reminded me from John 11:25 and 40 that He is the resurrection and the life, and that if I just believed Him, I would glimpse His glory. And I did—when I was given the privilege of speaking to the hundreds of people who gathered for my friend's funeral service, and many responded by putting their trust in Jesus.

When I overheard my son and his first wife in that heated argument, God acknowledged my emotional turmoil, yet lifted the veil briefly through Isaiah 54:10–13 so that I caught a reflection of His glory in my family's future. While there is still more yet to come, I have already seen each family member reflect the glory of God in the most unexpected ways.

When I returned home with my children to a house that had been broken into by thieves, the Lord reminded me from Matthew 6:20 that my real treasures were safely in Heaven. While I enjoy material things, I have learned to hold them loosely, for I know that the real treasure is what's inside of me.

When I discovered my husband unresponsive in our pool, I jumped into the water, pulled his head up on my lap, and prayed Daniel's prayer as passionately, as desperately, as I ever have. I readily recalled a promise memorized in childhood: "God is our refuge and strength, an ever present help in trouble. Therefore we will not fear."[2] God quickly brought emergency responders to our aid. They were able to restart Danny's heart. As I followed Danny to the ER and then into ICU, I had complete peace that was like a river deep within.

Two days later, with my precious children and their spouses surrounding Danny's bed, I gave permission to the hospital medical team to remove him from life support. They did, and with a flood of tears running down our faces, we sang to him, read Scripture to him, and praised the God of Heaven who is always good, loving, faithful . . . and who knows best. As Danny took his last breath, I claimed out loud the promises in Revelation 21 and 22: Danny had passed from death to real life. He was in the presence of his Lord and Savior. He was finally Home. And I will see him again.

Later, my inner peace was challenged as I agonized in reflection on what to me seemed like a horrific accident. God directed me to Isaiah 25:1—"O Lord, you are my God; I will exalt you and praise your name, for in perfect faithfulness you have done marvelous things, things planned long ago." I know to this day that my husband's death was not an accident. It was God's foreordained time for him to move to our Father's House. And so my heart has been filled not only with peace, but with praise for His perfect faithfulness to carry out to completion what He had begun in Danny's life seventy-eight years prior.[3] Danny had finished his race.[4]

Daniel knew what it was to open up the Scriptures and pray according to the promises he found in God's Word. He "understood from the Scriptures, according to the word of the LORD given to Jeremiah the prophet, that the desolation of Jerusalem would last seventy years" (9:2).

The promise he discovered during his Bible reading in Jeremiah gave Daniel insight in how to pray for his people. It was also a promise that Daniel proceeded to claim personally on behalf of his people.

PROMISES THAT ARE PERSONAL

God still speaks to us personally through His Word. The morning I wrote this chapter, I was reading my *Daily Light*, a small volume I have read since my mother gave me my first copy at ten years of age.[5] It consists of a compilation of Scriptures for both morning and evening. As I read the morning portion, verse after verse "leaped up off the page," and I knew God was speaking to me. Let me explain.

I had just been in prayer, telling the Lord that I wasn't sure how much longer I could continue caring for my husband while overseeing my ministry and writing books. But this is how the Lord spoke to me in response to my heart's cry: *Be strong . . . and work; for I am with you. . . . Be strong in the Lord and in the power of His might. . . . Let your hands be strong, you who have been hearing in these days these words by the mouth of the prophets* [Daniel]. *. . . Go in this might of yours. . . . Therefore, since* [you] *have this ministry, as* [you] *have received mercy,* [you] *do not lose heart. . . .* [Don't] *grow weary while doing good, for in due season* [you] *shall reap if* [you] *do not lose heart.*[6]

What encouragement that gave me! What a total lift

to my spirit! And I knew God was giving me insight in how to pray for myself.

God speaks personally to us through His Word, but we need to learn to listen to His voice.[7] One way is to pray before you read your Bible. Talk to God about what's on your heart and mind. Then open His Word and "listen" with your eyes on the page. He may not speak to you every time you read it, but He will speak.

You and I will never know how to storm the gates of Heaven until we start listening for God. A dramatic example of this is found in Genesis 6.

One day, God spoke to Noah, revealing that He was going to destroy the world because it was so permeated with wickedness. But then He also revealed salvation from judgment. And He told Noah specifically what to do about it: he was to build an ark as a means of salvation for the human race and the animal kingdom. Noah claimed God's promise by doing everything exactly as God said. As a result he, his family, and the human race were saved.[8]

Like Noah, Abraham also walked with God, indicating a personal, interactive relationship. When God shared His intention of destroying Sodom and Gomorrah, Abraham was deeply concerned because his nephew Lot lived in Sodom. So Abraham began to intercede for Sodom, asking God to spare it for the sake of the righteous who lived there. God did not find enough righteous people to justify withholding judgment, but when He destroyed the two cities, He went out of His way to save Lot and his family in answer to Abraham's intense, persistent prayer.[9]

When you and I storm the gates of Heaven, pleading with God according to His Word, someone else's salvation may depend on it. So how do you read your Bible? Do you read it to increase your knowledge of the facts only? Or do you read it listening expectantly for God to speak to you, then talk to Him about what He has said, basing your prayers on it? Start the habit of reading your Bible each day and highlighting promises or phrases that you can use as the basis of your prayers.

It's a habit that was held by two of the women whom God used to help shape my life. One was Miss A. Wetherell Johnson, the founder and director of Bible Study Fellowship. She taught and trained me to teach the Bible with accuracy, with balance, and with a heart of passionate love for the Author as well as the audience.

My last conversation with her was on the phone. I knew, unless God miraculously intervened, that she would soon lose her battle with cancer. I wanted to call her but didn't know what I would say. Still, I wanted desperately to hear her voice one more time. So I got up the courage and called. To this day, I'm embarrassed to admit that when I heard her weakened English accent, I became emotional and blurted out the most ridiculous thing I could have said: "Miss Johnson, how are you?"

Remarkably, she understood my heart and didn't

address my painfully obvious question. Instead, she told me she spent her days trying to overcome the pain while thanking God for medication. Next she said, "I've just been reading the life of Jacob once again, and I learned . . ." Her voice trailed off and I didn't catch what she had learned! Sensing her fatigue, I couldn't bear to ask her to repeat herself. But what I learned is that at the end of her life, she was still reading her Bible and being taught new things!

The other woman whose love for God's Word greatly impacted my life was my own mother. Indelibly impressed on my mind is the picture of Mother toward the end of her life as she sat on her bed, unable to walk or get around easily because of arthritic pain in her back and hips, yet with eyes sparkling as her hands held her big black Bible. Because of her macular degeneration, she could no longer read that Bible, but she was memorizing scripture (Romans 8) that her assistant had typed out for her in large, two-inch block letters.

Both Miss Johnson and my mother were in their eighties, the same age Daniel was when he recorded his prayer. No wonder all three of them prayed in such a way that the promises of God were fulfilled.[10] Their prayers emerged and blossomed from the depths of God's Word.

If our prayers are not rooted in what God has said, what is their basis? A wish? A want? A hope-so? Prayer that claims the promises of God, changing your life and mine, is based on God's Word. If you have a specific need, want, wish, or hope, put it in the form of a request, then open your Bible and ask God to speak to you about it. He may change the way you are praying, as He did with me. Or He may confirm the way you are praying.

Ask Him for a promise on which you can base your prayer. A promise for whatever is uppermost on your mind. Then pray. God loves to be held to His Word.

For instance, just as I was reviewing this section of the manuscript, my daughter Rachel-Ruth called. Her voice was breathless. I could tell she was holding back her emotions. As she told me how God had just spoken to her, I understood why. She shared that as she was fixing breakfast for her girls, she had turned on the television news and was reminded that one year previous to the day, 276 Nigerian girls had been kidnapped by the terrorist group Boko Haram. After she had driven her children to school, she had come back to the house and opened her Bible to work on the message she was going to give to her class, about Paul's experience of getting swept up into a dangerous storm that resulted in a shipwreck. Her eye fell on Acts 27:37, which reports that "altogether there were 276 of us on board," then in verse 44, "everyone reached land in safety."

To Rachel-Ruth's consternation and amazement, the number of kidnapped girls matched exactly the number of lives endangered on Paul's ship during the storm. Using this "divine coincidence" as a catalyst, she immediately felt that God in Heaven was alerting her to pray for the girls. And although I knew she had already prayed, we prayed together over the phone for the girls that we knew had Heaven's undivided attention at that moment.

When God burdens us with what burdens Him, our responsibility is to pray. Then we leave the answer up to Him. And who knows? Across the ocean, deep in the heart of Africa, back in the jungle, were the girls comforted with a sudden awareness of God's love and His presence? Did they have a flash of hope, knowing inexplicably that they were not forgotten? That they were on God's mind and He would deliver them one day and bring them Home, either to their parents or to their Heavenly Father? Were they given the strength to make it through one more day, all because Rachel-Ruth paid attention and prayed?

While you and I may not have as dramatic a word from the Lord, the principle is the same. God speaks to us through His Word, and it's His Word that we need to "speak" back to Him in prayer.

Promises That Are Conditional

God's Word gives strength to our feeble prayers, doesn't it? Which is one reason why Daniel's prayer is so powerful. It flowed from God's Word.

The promise that Daniel came across in his Bible reading was Jeremiah 29:10–14 . . .

"This is what the LORD says: 'When seventy years are completed for Babylon, I will come to you and fulfill my gracious promise to bring you back to this place. . . . Then you will call upon me and come and pray to me, and I will listen to you. You will seek me and find me when you seek me with all your heart. I will be found by you,' declares the LORD, 'and will bring you back from captivity. I will gather you from all the nations and places where I have banished you,' declares the LORD, 'and will bring you back to the place from which I carried you into exile.'"

When Daniel read those verses, I wonder if he rubbed his eyes, then reread them. Did this mean that in three years the captives would all be going home? *Back to Jerusalem?*

He must surely have been thrilled beyond words by this incredible thought. But then . . . was there a small whisper in his heart? Did he go back to reread Jeremiah, this time not looking for the promises, but for any conditions that needed to be met in order to receive those promises? There they were! . . . *Then you will call upon me and come and pray to me, and I will listen to you. You will seek me and find me when you seek me with all your heart.*

One promise for our nation that has been prayed frequently comes from 2 Chronicles 7:13–15. If a promise could be worn out from use, this one might be tattered beyond recognition. But promises cannot be worn out. They are like gold. They don't even tarnish. In fact, the more we claim them, the more they seem to "glow" with even greater meaning. Then why has this one not made more of a difference in our nation? Could it be that we have given little attention to the conditions attached to this promise? We must humble ourselves. Pray. Seek God's face. *And turn from our wicked ways.*

What difference would it make if we claimed the promise while also meeting the condition for receiving it? Like Daniel, I want to find out. So with the condition in mind, let's take a moment and pray 2 Chronicles 7:13–15 together:

Lord of mercy, God of grace, hear us as we pray. You have promised that if, when environmental disasters erupt, or the enemy strikes, or illnesses break out, we Your people, who call ourselves by Your name would set aside our pride and self-righteousness and make the time to get alone with You to pray—seeking not just a political solution but Your face, turning from our own grievous sin—then Heaven would be moved! Sin would be forgiven! Hearts would be changed! And you would bless our land!

*So now we humbly confess to You our sin of
_____, and _____, and _____.
We name it for what it is in Your sight, and choose to
put it out of our lives. To turn away from it. We ask
You to cleanse us with the blood of Your Son and our
Savior. Hear our prayer. Forgive us our sin. Open
Your eyes to our beloved nation. Answer us according
to Your Word, for the glory of Your Name. Amen.*

CHAPTER 3

CENTERED
IN PRAYER

Having been raised in the Blue Ridge Mountains of western North Carolina, I have always loved to hike. When I was young, my entire family, including one or more dogs, would hike to the ridge behind our home every Sunday afternoon.

When we made it to the end of the old logging road, we'd hike the last several hundred feet on a trail choked with underbrush that required walking single file. Daddy always went first. I knew if I kept my eyes on him, eventually I would come out to the bare place on top of the mountain where we could see all the way down the Swannanoa Valley to Asheville.

Just as it's necessary to have a center point when hiking in thick woods, you and I need a center point when we pray. Daniel's faith was centered on the living God. Before Daniel even gives us the words of his prayer, he makes it clear that he "turned to the Lord God" (9:3). He set his compass on God as his True North. To do this helps me as well.

Years ago, I adopted the habit of beginning virtually every prayer I pray with worship. As I center on the One to whom I'm speaking, I try to think of the specific attributes of His character that are relevant to my prayer. For instance, if I'm burdened for my children, I address God as my Heavenly Father, worshiping Him as a parent who is supremely patient, loving, good, yet has children that are not perfect. He understands parental agony and heartbreak.

If I'm hurt and wounded, I address Him as the One who was wounded for my transgressions, who understands the feelings of my pain and has promised to heal my broken heart. If I have just been blessed or honored, I address Him as the Fountainhead of all blessing, the Giver of every good thing. If I am coming to Him aware that I've sinned, before even confessing it to Him, I worship Him as the God of mercy and grace who stands ready to pardon and cleanse all those who come to Him by faith at the foot of the Cross.

It's amazing how the simple exercise of putting my focus on who God is helps put my prayers into perspective. My problems don't seem so overwhelming. My questions don't seem so critical. My worries don't seem so all-consuming. Centering on Him brings peace and calm to my spirit. In the quietness I very often hear His whisper as He directs me out of the thick underbrush.

On the other hand, if I begin my prayer focusing on

the doctor's grim prognosis for my loved one,
the probability of a conflict with my child's
    teacher,
the impact of the company downsizing my job,
the increasing prevalence of active shooters, or
the raw savagery of radical militant jihadists . . .

I become overwhelmed to the point that I have no faith whatsoever that my prayers will make any difference at all. My worries and fears appear to be inevitable. The enemy just seems too powerful. The result? I get lost emotionally and spiritually.

When do you set your compass? Do you turn to others before you turn to the Lord God? Daniel's prayer has helped me refocus when I talk with God.

PRIVACY MATTERS
WHEN WE PRAY

When Daniel turned to God, it's implied that he turned away from everyone and everything else so that he could pray privately.

Privacy in prayer matters.

Jesus emphasized it to His disciples in the Sermon on the Mount: "When you pray, go into your room, close the door and pray to your Father, who is unseen."[1] Then He set a personal example: "Jesus often withdrew to lonely places and prayed."[2]

There is no denying that when Jesus prayed, Heaven was moved and things on earth changed. Which leads me to wonder, if you only pray when you are with others or you are in church, how effective and active is your prayer life? Isn't it time for you to draw aside to get alone with God?

Luke's Gospel tells us that Jesus took three of His disciples—Peter, James, and John—up a high mountain. As He was praying there, His clothes became dazzling white, as brilliant as a flash of lightning. His face shone with the brilliance of the sun—and the light was not being reflected from anything. The light was coming from within Jesus. The disciples were seeing Him transfigured in His glory as the Son of God, the glory that He had laid aside when He had become the Son of Man.[3] But what followed is a lesson that God has driven down deep into my heart.

When Jesus and the three disciples went back down the mountain into the valley, they were met by a small riot. People were arguing with each other and with the religious leaders. When Jesus inquired what was going on, a man stepped out from the mob. He explained that he had brought his son, who was totally out of control, to Jesus's disciples for help. But they had been unable to help him.

Jesus rebuked His disciples for their lack of faith, then He healed the boy. Later, when His disciples asked Him why they had been unable to help, Jesus replied, "This kind can come out by nothing but prayer and fasting."[4]

Had Jesus invited all twelve of His disciples to draw aside with Him for a time of private prayer? Did only three of them accept His invitation? Did the other nine give excuses such as: "I don't have time"; "My family needs me this weekend"; "I'm too busy in ministry"; "Climbing that mountain is hard work—I'm too tired"; "I have other things to do"?

For whatever reason, the critical truth is that the nine who did not make the effort to draw aside in private prayer with Jesus on the mountain had no power to help others in the valley. And so I have asked myself, *If my prayer doesn't move Heaven or change the world, could it be that I have not spent time with Jesus—in private prayer?*

Modern life is not conducive to private prayer, is it? If your days are like mine, they're full to the brim. If I waited until I had the time to draw aside and pray, I doubt I would ever pray. So I have to make the time for private prayer.

To be honest, I'm afraid not to. I don't want to miss out on the power that's necessary to really help others. I don't want to miss out on the power that's necessary to impact the world around me.

While I know that I can pray any time and any place, in front of thousands or in a circle of dozens, I also know that there are times I need to be alone, free of distractions and interruptions. Just by myself. With my Heavenly Father.

SINCERITY MATTERS WHEN WE PRAY

Forsaking everything to get alone with God and pray is a form of fasting. *Fasting* simply means to "go without" to make time to pray. We associate it most often with abstaining from food, but it can also be abstinence from emails, phone calls, entertainment, web surfing, meetings, housework, shopping, cooking, talking—the list is unlimited. While in prayer we *turn to* God, in fasting we *turn away* from everything else.

Fasting is not a "work" we add to our prayer effort to

merit His answer—His answers are gifts of His grace, not rewards for our work. It is not to make God love us more or pay us more attention—He loves us completely, fully; He can't love us any more. And He has already given us His undivided attention without our fasting. So why do we fast?

One reason is because Jesus expects it. He told His disciples, "*When* you fast . . ."[5] For myself, fasting has helped to purify my motives in prayer. It sharpens my focus on Heavenly things and clarifies my perspective on earthly things. And perhaps most importantly, it reveals how sincere I am as I seek the Lord.

Have you ever fasted from anything? Daniel "turned to the Lord God and pleaded with him . . . in fasting" (9:3). I suggest you start to build fasting into your prayer life, if you haven't already. Talk to God about it, then decide what you will fast from, when you will fast from it, and how long you will maintain your fast. Then do it. Discover for yourself the difference it makes.

I first discovered the power of fasting when my husband, Danny, and I decided we wanted children. In my naïveté I thought all I had to do was to stop using birth control and babies would start coming. I was wrong. Month after month, my womb would empty out. I went to specialists who assured me nothing was wrong, but they couldn't tell me why I did not get pregnant.

I shared my grief with my very wise mother, who responded, "Anne, if more mothers prayed for their babies like Hannah prayed for hers, maybe we would have more Samuels." So I turned in my Bible and read about Hannah to learn what was so unique about her prayer life.[6]

Hannah wanted her own baby with such intensity that she wept and could no longer eat. She fasted from food. Then she fasted from everything when she went up to the temple to pray.

In answer to her prayer and fasting, God promised her a son. Soon after, she became pregnant and gave birth to Samuel, whom she dedicated to God. Samuel grew "in stature and in favor with the LORD and with men,"[7] becoming an exceedingly great man who was a prophet, judge, and kingmaker in Israel.

Following Hannah's example, I set aside one day each week to pray and fast for a son. One year after I turned to the Lord with deep sincerity on a regular basis, I seemed to hear God whispering to my heart, *Anne, you don't have to fast anymore. I will give you a baby.* I immediately stopped fasting and started praising God for having heard and answered my prayer. The next month, I conceived. Nine months later, I gave birth to our son, Jonathan.

Was I able to get pregnant and give birth because I had fasted? I honestly don't know. What I do know is that fasting changed me. By the end of that year of prayer and fasting, I was genuinely satisfied with the Lord and with my husband. If I had not gotten pregnant, if I had never had any children at all, I knew I would be okay.

Interestingly, it was when I let go and released my desire for a baby that I became pregnant. So, indirectly, fasting seemed to play a significant role, because without it, I don't believe I would have been able to release my all-consuming desire for a child.

HUMILITY MATTERS WHEN WE PRAY

Prayer that storms the gates of Heaven doesn't have to be fancy or long or filled with Bible verses. In fact, I almost wonder if it needs words at all. It really is a heart's cry, isn't it? And one wrapped in complete humility.

Recently, I spoke at a Christian gathering that was multigenerational, multiracial, and multidenominational. Before I spoke, a young pastor walked up to the platform to lead in prayer. With eyes wide open, walking back and forth, gesturing to the congregation, he didn't miss a beat as he "prayed."

He was smooth, dynamic, polished, articulate . . . and proud? I hesitate to say that because only God could see his heart, but he came across as being almost spiritually arrogant. Haughty. In his words, body language, and gestures, he seemed to be performing to impress instead of praying. And he certainly didn't lead me into

God's presence. In fact, the spirit within me recoiled. His "prayer" reminded me of a story Jesus told to those "who were confident of their own righteousness and looked down on everybody else."[8]

In His parable, Jesus describes two men who went up to the temple to pray.[9] One was a Pharisee, a highly educated leader in Israel who was so scrupulous in keeping all the nuances, regulations, and traditions of his religion that he was considered exemplary. The other was a tax collector who was considered a low-life because, although a Jew, he collaborated with the occupying Romans for pay.

So Jesus described these two men from God's perspective. The Pharisee "stood up and prayed about himself," saying, "God, I thank you that I am not like other men—or even like this tax collector. I fast twice a week and give a tenth of all I get." By contrast, the tax collector "stood at a distance. He would not even look up to heaven, but beat his breast and said, 'God, have mercy on me, a sinner.'"

In the event that someone listening didn't understand His meaning, Jesus summarized His story, "I tell you that this man [the tax collector], rather than the other [the Pharisee], went home justified before God. For everyone who exalts himself will be humbled, and he who humbles himself will be exalted."

God doesn't just listen to our words when we pray. He's not impressed at all with our reputation, who we think we are or who others think we are. He looks on the heart. In case there is any doubt, Proverbs clearly states, "The LORD detests all the proud of heart."[10] On the other hand, God confirms, "This is the one I esteem: he who is humble and contrite in spirit, and trembles at my word."[11]

In other words, someone like Daniel.

As we have already seen, he quickly rose through the ranks of officials in Nebuchadnezzar's court until he was ruler over Babylon.[12] Daniel held this high position under three more emperors in three successive empires: Belshazzar, who briefly ruled in Babylon; Darius, who destroyed the Babylonians and ushered in the Medo-Persian Empire; and finally Cyrus, who eliminated the Medes and set up the Persian Empire. In anyone's estimation, Daniel was a very great, important, powerful man.

It was obvious that he was a very great, important, powerful man in Heaven's estimation too. God revealed to Daniel the dreams of others, as well as what the dreams meant. Angels personally delivered God's answers to Daniel's prayers. And God miraculously delivered him when his enemies contrived to feed him to lions. Yet as he began to pray, he smeared himself with "ashes" (9:3). He humbled himself. Because he knew humility matters to God.

It's interesting how pride can creep into our attitude when we pray, isn't it? We think if we keep all the "rules"—if we're good, moral, helpful, thoughtful—then somehow God owes us the answer we want. So after prayer, when our spouse walks out on us, or the doctor diagnoses us with a terminal illness, or a business partner betrays us, then we angrily feel God has somehow let us down.

When Danny and I first got married, we lived in a university town. Every Sunday night, we opened our home to student athletes for fellowship, Bible study, and prayer. Some were on football scholarship, while others were on the basketball and lacrosse teams. In addition we had two cheerleaders. Danny and I loved them all. And they loved us. I would fix a homemade pie or cake, and we would sit around eating the desserts and discussing the Scriptures.

I'll never forget a football player who came to our home one Sunday night very dejected. He was a huge offensive lineman. His team had played an archrival the day before. They had taken the football all the way down the field in the fourth quarter. The last play was fourth down with less than one yard to the goal line. Needing the six points a touchdown would give them for victory, they went for it.

The tough lineman told us that as they broke the huddle, he had prayed to God, asking His help for them to power the ball over the goal line. But the opposing team held them, and his team lost the game. Between bites of pie, the big football player hung his head and, with a dark look, shared that he felt God had let him down. We all tried to talk him through it, but he never came back to our home. To this day, I grieve over him.

If you are honest, would you say you are like the big lineman? Do you think God has let you down in some way? Could it be that there is pride lurking like a cobweb in the dark inner recesses of your heart? Pride that suggests God owes you something? That you deserve better? That you deserve anything? Maybe it's time you smeared yourself with ashes.

With a laser-like focus centered on the Lord, Daniel began to plead with God privately, in utmost sincerity, and with deep, genuine humility. And that's where the prayer that storms Heaven's gates and claims God's promises begins . . .

PART 2

PLEADING IN PRAYER

Rend your heart and not your garments. Return to the Lord your God, for he is gracious and compassionate, slow to anger and abounding in love, and he relents from sending calamity. Who knows? He may turn and have pity and leave behind a blessing.

JOEL 2:13–14

CHAPTER 4

PLEADING WITH CONFIDENCE

Is faith a gift that some people have been given and others have not? No, faith is a choice.

There's an old story, a favorite of mine, about a veteran tightrope walker who, after demonstrating he could push a wheelbarrow filled with sand across Niagara Falls on a tightrope, asked the applauding crowd for a volunteer. No one moved. Finally, a little old man in the back raised his hand, stepped forward, and offered, "I've seen what you've done, and I've heard what you've said. I believe you can push me across, so I'll do it."

Everyone in the crowd held their breath and strained to watch as the wheelbarrow was rolled over the falls and back again. On the final return, the roar of the crowd was deafening as the old man emerged from the wheelbarrow. The acrobat gallantly bowed, saluted, smiled broadly, and said, "Thank you, sir, for your faith in me."

The point of the story, of course, is that while everyone in the crowd had said they believed the tightrope walker *could* carry a man across the falls in his wheelbarrow, only the little old man demonstrated real faith by climbing into the wheelbarrow. Real faith is more than just words or rituals or going to church or believing there is a God. Real faith backs up words with actions.[1] By choice.

CONFIDENT FAITH IS A CHOICE

Daniel is Exhibit A of a man who demonstrated real faith in his choices. He not only said he believed, but he backed up his words with death-defying actions. We are not told when he originally chose to believe, but all indications are that it was during his early years growing up in Jerusalem. By the time he walked on the stage of world history as a teenager, his faith seemed remarkably well developed.

Daniel's first death-defying act recorded in Scripture took place when he arrived in Babylon. In an effort to uproot him from his past and remold him according to Nebuchadnezzar's pleasure, he was immediately plunged into an intense, three-year brainwashing regimen. Daniel was stripped of his Hebrew name, which meant "God is my judge." The new name assigned to him, Belteshazzar, was intended to give him a Babylonian identity, one paying tribute to a pagan Babylonian god.

At the same time, more than likely, he was also stripped of his masculinity, since his immediate supervisor was described as the "master of [the] eunuchs," implying Daniel was one (1:3 NKJV). This was surely intended to force Daniel into a subservient position of humiliation, underscoring that he would have no personal life at all; his only purpose was to serve Nebuchadnezzar.

While it was impossible for Daniel to prevent the changing of his name or his emasculation, he drew the line at being forced to eat the king's food that had first been sacrificed to idols. To do so was an indirect way of giving tribute to them and effectively denying his own God. So he "resolved not to defile himself with the royal food and wine, and he asked the chief official for permission not to defile himself this way" (1:8).

Although Ashpenaz, the chief eunuch, personally liked Daniel, he reacted strongly, explaining that to reject the food assigned by the king himself was to place all of their lives in grave danger. Daniel could so easily have told God, *Well, I tried. You know in my heart I'm not giving tribute to these gods, but I have to survive.* But Daniel did not back down. Not even a little. Having made the choice not to defile himself, the only alternative he could think of was to place his life in God's hands. So Daniel went to his guard and suggested a test: Serve me and my three friends a different diet, free of the association with pagan gods. After ten days, if we are not better off than the other young captives who eat the king's food, you can do whatever you choose (which implied the guard could execute them all for insubordination).

Ten days later, Daniel and his friends Meshach, Shadrach, and Abednego "looked healthier and better nourished than any of the young men who ate the royal food" (1:15). They remained on that diet, and three years later, when the king himself gave them their final exams, these young men were found to be ten times better off than all their advisors and professors.

Daniel had put God to the test. God came through for him in such a way that Daniel's faith surely grew. Which was a very good thing, because his faith was again tested when King Nebuchadnezzar had a series of deeply disturbing dreams. The king threatened to kill every wise man in the kingdom unless someone could both interpret what he'd dreamed and describe what he dreamed.

None of his counselors could do so, But when Daniel learned of the situation, he requested an audience with the king. Surely bolstered by his earlier experience of

God's faithfulness, Daniel once again acted on his faith in the living God. And once again, God came through.

By the morning light God had given Daniel the dream and the interpretation. When Daniel went to the king, Nebuchadnezzar's eyes must have narrowed as he skeptically asked, "Are you able to tell me what I saw in my dream and interpret it?" (2:26). Daniel's fearless answer reveals his rocklike confidence in God: "No wise man, enchanter, magician or diviner can explain to the king the mystery he has asked about, but there is a God in heaven who reveals mysteries. He has shown King Nebuchadnezzar what will happen in days to come" (2:27–28). Then Daniel proceeded to describe the dream and its meaning.

The king was astounded! More significantly, God was glorified as Nebuchadnezzar acknowledged that Daniel's God is the God of gods and the Lord of kings. And Daniel was honored by being made ruler over all of Babylon.

It was during the reign of Darius that Daniel was given perhaps his most dramatic opportunity to climb into the wheelbarrow.

Darius appointed Daniel as one of his three top officials. But Daniel was so exceptional that Darius planned to make him second in command over the entire kingdom. The other rulers were jealous and began a private investigation of Daniel in hopes of finding something they could smear him with in the eyes of the king. They found nothing, except that three times a day Daniel went into his upstairs room, opened his window toward Jerusalem, and prayed.

The rulers went to Darius with flattering words and convinced him to issue a decree that people could only pray to him. Being fed to starving lions would be the penalty for disobedience.

Daniel didn't flinch. As always, he opened his window toward Jerusalem and continued praying three times a day. Sure enough, his enemies saw this and ran gleefully to report to the king.

Darius was genuinely distressed because Daniel held great favor with him, and yet the law he had signed into effect was irrevocable. So Daniel, the man of God who had served Babylon and Persia with such exceptional distinction, was thrown into the lions' den as the king himself uttered a type of prayer: "May your God, whom you serve continually, rescue you!" (6:16). The king himself seemed to "catch" Daniel's bold, confident faith—because faith is contagious, isn't it?

CONFIDENT FAITH IS CONTAGIOUS

Darius tossed and turned all night. He could not eat and he could not sleep. Early the next morning, Darius ran to the lions' den, calling out, "Daniel, . . . has your

God, whom you serve continually, been able to rescue you from the lions?' Daniel answered, 'O king, live forever! My God sent his angel, and he shut the mouths of the lions. They have not hurt me'" (6:20–22).

The overjoyed Darius scooped Daniel up out of the den and immediately executed the men who had hatched the plot. He then proceeded to issue a decree that everyone in his kingdom was to fear and reverence the God of Daniel. Listen to Darius' testimony: "He is the living God and he endures forever; his kingdom will not be destroyed, his dominion will never end" (6:26). God was glorified!

Which makes me wonder what my choices really reveal. When I pray, *God, be glorified in my life,* do I truly mean it? If you and I rarely exercise our faith, how can we be surprised when it's too weak to be contagious?

CONFIDENT FAITH IN GOD'S COVENANT

With years of experience to back him up, Daniel knew when he prayed that he was speaking to a living Person who would listen and respond. Even more, Daniel was supremely confident that the living God of the universe was committed to him. He had established a personal, covenant relationship with the God of Abraham, Isaac, and Jacob. This confidence comes through clearly when he relates, "I prayed to the LORD *my* God . . ." (9:4, emphasis mine). Daniel knew that God was his, and he was God's. And it was this covenant relationship with God that is the bedrock of Daniel's prayer.

While God can hear and answer any prayer He chooses, when you and I come to Him in a covenant relationship, we are guaranteed He will listen to us and answer. So, before beginning the actual words of Daniel's prayer, it's to our benefit to determine if we are in a covenant relationship with God. Are you? I am.

My confidence is based on the choice I made when I was eight or nine years of age, to place my trust in Jesus as my Savior and Lord. Although with my child's mind I didn't understand the full scope of my choice at the time, looking back I know that's when I entered into a covenant relationship with God.

A covenant is a legal agreement between two or more parties, as in a treaty between nations. Or a land covenant between the buyer and the seller of property. Or a marriage covenant between husband and wife. The old biblical covenant with God is the one Daniel entered into through the Jewish laws, ceremonies, and sacrifices.

The new covenant I entered into is one that Jesus established by fulfilling the old covenant perfectly through His life and death. I entered into the new covenant as I "drank the cup" of His blood, claiming His sacrifice on the Cross to make atonement for my sin, and as I "ate the bread" of His body when I took Him into my heart and gave Him access to every part of my life. The incredible, glorious truth is that once I entered into a covenant relationship with Him, He entered into that relationship with me, and I am His. Forever.

A covenant relationship with God is the equivalent of a legal promise to which He binds Himself so that you and I can take Him at His word with absolute confidence. It's His guarantee—*signed with His own blood*.

When have you entered into that covenant? Don't hope that you have. Don't think that you have. You must *know* that you have if you are going to storm the gates of Heaven with prayer that claims the promises of God. If you are not sure . . . make sure. Right now. Pray something like this:

Lord God,

Thank You for inviting me to enter into a covenant with You. I earnestly desire to be assured that You are committed to me forever. I long to belong to You. So right now, I confess to You that I am a sinner and have no merit of my own to deserve or earn this privilege. I confess to you my _____ [fill in the blank with specific sins that come to your mind]. I'm willing to turn away from my sin. To stop sinning. But I need Your help.

Please forgive me and cleanse me of all my sin and guilt. I believe Jesus died on the Cross for me and rose up from the dead to give me eternal life. I surrender every part of my life to His authority. Please come into my heart and be Lord of my life.

Thank You for hearing this prayer. I take You at Your word. I climb into the wheelbarrow and trust myself to You completely. Forever. Amen.[2]

Signed: _____

Date: _____

Praise God! You are eternally secured! The covenant does not depend on your ability to "keep" it, but on the living God's ability to keep you. Jesus made it clear that no one can ever take you from your Father's hand.[3]

Now that you are confident of your covenant relationship with God, you too can pray to the Lord *your* God, knowing that He will hear your prayer and answer you. What an awesome privilege!

CONFIDENT FAITH IN GOD'S CHARACTER

Daniel was not only confident in his covenant relationship with God, but he was confident in God's character. He knew the Person to whom he was speaking.

Daniel's prayer begins dramatically with a declaration of praise for who God is. It addresses God with awe and wonder as well as tenderness and intimacy. It reminds us that when we pray, we are actually communicating with a living Person who has . . .

eyes to see us,

ears to hear us,

feet that swiftly come to our aid,

hands to hold us,

a mind that thinks on us,

and a heart to love us.

What a difference it makes in my perspective and in my spirit when I make the time to center on who God is before I pour out my list of complaints or problems or needs or worries. Focusing on the character of the One to whom I am speaking calms my spirit, lifts my eyes, and encourages my faith as I begin to pray.

And faith is a necessity if our prayers are going to move Heaven. The Bible says that when we come to God in prayer, we must believe that He is who He says He is, and that He will answer our prayer when we earnestly seek Him.[4]

His Faithfulness

As Daniel began to pray, at the forefront of his mind were the experiences he had had over his eighty-plus years of God's faithfulness to him. God had allowed Daniel to be kidnapped, enslaved, emasculated, endangered, threatened, betrayed, accused, and fed to lions! BUT God had never forsaken him. It's no wonder that Daniel began his prayer with worship of God for His faithfulness: "O Lord, the great and awesome God, who keeps his covenant of love with all who love him and keep his commandments" (9:4).

What experiences have you had of God's faithfulness? Have you been so focused on the tragedies or the troubles, the struggles or the setbacks, that you've lost sight of God's faithfulness to be right there with you, then bring you through? Take a few moments and reflect on your life. Make a list of the times you have glimpsed God's faithfulness to you, then praise Him.

Jeremiah, whose book Daniel had been reading when he was prompted to pray, bore witness to hard times. He had preached for over sixty years, warning his people of God's imminent judgment if they did not repent. As far as we know, he never received even one positive response to his message. And in the end, he saw his prophecies fulfilled when Nebuchadnezzar destroyed Jerusalem. Jeremiah wrote a very moving testimony: "I remember my affliction and my wandering, the bitterness and the gall. I well remember them, and my soul is downcast within me. Yet this I call to mind and therefore I have hope. Because of the LORD's great love we are not consumed, for his compassions never fail. They are new every morning; great is your faithfulness."[5]

His Righteousness

As Daniel reflected on how all the dire, prophetic warnings of impending judgment had been fulfilled to even the smallest detail, he was confident that God had done the right thing. Instead of expressing bitterness, anger, or offense with God for allowing evil to have the upper hand, Daniel prayed, "Lord, you are righteous" (9:7).

Not only was Daniel acknowledging the "rightness" of God's dealings with his nation, but he was acknowledging God's rightness in the way He had dealt with Daniel. Think of Daniel's suffering. His separation from family and loved ones. His slavery. The stripping of his identity. His success that constantly seemed to be challenged. In light of what God had allowed him to go through, Daniel's absolute confidence in the righteousness of God seems amazing.

Would you and I honestly say the same thing? What about

if you were fired from your job . . .

if your spouse walked out . . .

if you were diagnosed with a deadly disease . . .

if your reputation was destroyed . . .

if your retirement evaporated . . .

if a car accident left you paralyzed . . .

if you went through what Daniel went through, would you be tempted as Job was, to "curse God and die"?[6] Or would you pray as Daniel prayed?

How can you and I truly believe that God does the

right thing when really wrong things happen to us, our loved ones, our nation, and our world? We can confidently say so because God is righteous. That's His character. He never does the wrong thing. He cannot be anything other than Himself.

And He is righteous. All the time.

His Goodness

All the way back in the Garden of Eden, Satan tempted the first woman, Eve, to doubt the goodness of God. She lived in Paradise, literally, and was the adored wife of the first man, Adam. She could have had anything she wanted. Except for one thing. She had been forbidden to eat the fruit from the tree of the knowledge of good and evil. The restriction was God's test of the first couple's love and devotion to Him.

The test intensified when Satan slithered up and suggested to Eve, "God knows that when you eat of it your eyes will be opened, and you will be like God, knowing good and evil."[7]

Eve failed the test miserably. She bought into the argument that God was holding out on her. That He really isn't a good God. So she and Adam both ate the forbidden fruit, blatantly disobeying what God had said. As a result, her eyes were opened, but in a way God never intended. She knew good, but she now knew she was separated from it. And she knew evil, because she was saturated in it.

As a further result, sin and death came into the human race. And into Eve's own family. She lived to witness her firstborn son, Cain, murder her second-born son, Abel. I can only imagine how many moments of how many days of how many years of the rest of her life Eve struggled with, "If only . . ." "If only I had obeyed God's word." "If only I had trusted God's goodness." "If only I had had confidence in God's character . . ."

What unjust or tragic or hurtful or evil thing has happened to you? Something that was unexpected, unwanted, unplanned. In the midst of the emotional wreckage, did Satan slither up beside you and hiss into your ear, *God is mean. He can't be trusted. He could have prevented this. He's out to get you. Do you remember the sin you committed . . . ? Well, He remembers. This is payback. Because God is not good.*

If you have the slightest suspicion that God is holding out on you . . .

If you have the slightest doubt that He wants what's best for you . . .

If you have even the slightest doubt that God is truly good . . .

you will struggle to storm the gates of Heaven with your prayers. You will lack confidence in the character of the One to whom you are praying. And that will make a huge impact on the effectiveness of your prayers.

So take a moment now to pinpoint your doubt of God's goodness and your reasons for it. Tell Him why you are afraid to get in the wheelbarrow and trust Him completely. Ask Him to give you experiences, as He did Daniel, that will help to build your confidence in Him. Then open your eyes to look past the experiences to the God who is behind them—and the greater purpose He has in mind.

His Greatness

As Daniel continued to pray, he reflected on God's power: "Now, Lord our God, who brought your people out of Egypt with a mighty hand . . . ," You've "made for yourself a name that endures to this day" (9:15).

God's name is synonymous with greatness. And other than Creation and the resurrection of Jesus Christ, there has never been a greater demonstration of God's power than when He delivered His people from slavery in Egypt.[8]

He appointed Moses, who had been born to Hebrew parents but, in a miraculous turn of events, was raised in the king's palace by the daughter of Pharaoh. He sent a series of plagues to Egypt. In the end, of course, Pharaoh relented and let God's people go. It's estimated that approximately two million Hebrew men, women, and children walked out of Egypt, led by Moses.

But the plagues were not the greatest demonstration of God's power. The parting of the Red Sea was, where God miraculously and mightily delivered His people from Pharoah's army. "When the Israelites saw the great power the LORD displayed against the Egyptians, the people feared the LORD and put their trust in him."[9]

As Daniel recalled this supreme, historic demonstration of God's unparalleled power to set His people free, he was compelled to plead with God, *Do it again!* If God had been moved to action as a result of the cries of the Israelite slaves in Egypt, surely the same God would be moved to action as a result of the cries of the Israelite slaves in Babylon.

And if God heard the cries of His people in Egypt and in Persia so that Heaven was moved to answer, why would He not hear our prayers today?

He can, can't He?

CHAPTER 5

PLEADING WITH CONFESSION

We called my paternal grandfather "Daddy Graham." He was a tall, soft-spoken, true Southern gentleman. He wore black-and-white spectator shoes and a broad-brimmed hat pulled down on his brow, but only when he was going to church or to the nearby S&W Cafeteria. For most of the week, he dressed in faded, well-worn work clothes that carried with them the "sweet essence of agriculture" because he was a dairy farmer.

Daddy Graham also grew the corn that he used to

feed his cows. After the corn was harvested, the bare ground of that cornfield hardened, and weeds and grass would begin to take over. Before Daddy Graham could plant the next crop of corn the following spring, he'd have to plow up the fallow earth so it would be soft enough to receive new seed and absorb the rain and sunshine that would follow.

The nation of Judah had once been a fertile field that had grown "crops" of righteousness—people who loved, obeyed, and served the Lord. But because of her sin, Daniel and his people were removed from their home and enslaved in a foreign land. In essence, the land and the people had lain "fallow" for sixty-seven years.

So Daniel's prayer was a plea for God to . . .

Plow up the fallow ground.
Forgive his people for their sins.
Release his people from judgment.
"Heal the land" and put God back at the center of their national life by reviving authentic worship and restoring the temple in Jerusalem.

And confession was key. Out of the sixteen verses covered by Daniel's prayer in chapter nine, twelve of them confess sin. Not "their" sin, but "our" sin. All through his prayer, Daniel uses plural pronouns. Which reveals to me that he was as aware of sin in his own heart as he was in the hearts of his people.

We may never have another Great Awakening in our own nation until you and I stop pointing our finger at "them" and deal with the sin in our own hearts and lives. An old-timey revivalist, Gypsy Smith, was asked where revival begins. He answered, *I draw a circle around myself and make sure everything in that circle is right with God.* Which prompts the question: If we have yet to see revival fire fall in our nation, could the problem be within the circle? Could the problem be with you and me?

CONFESSION OF PERSONAL SIN

Before leading a seminar several years ago, I set aside ten days to work on the seven different messages that I would be giving. On the first day, I pulled out my Bible, my pencil, and my legal pad, quickly prayed for God's blessing, then began to work through the passage of Scripture that would be the basis for the first message. As I sought to break open the passage, I got nothing. No real revelation or understanding at all. Concluding that weariness was dulling my mind, I put myself to bed.

The next morning, I felt refreshed. So I sat down at my desk where my Bible was still open from the night before, picked up my pen, and held it poised over the legal pad. Once again I prayed, this time with more expectancy. I then proceeded to read and reread the passage of Scripture. Nothing. I prayed again, except this time I explained to the Lord I only had a limited time to prepare the messages, hundreds of people arriving within nine days who had paid to hear them, and I needed His help.

Nothing.

And then, there seemed to be a small whisper in my heart. *Anne, I don't want to talk about the messages. I want to talk about you.* Recognizing the still, small voice of the Spirit, I replied honestly, *I don't want to talk about me. There's no time. I want to talk about these messages. After I have prepared and delivered them, then we will talk about me.*

Now there was dead silence that was becoming quite loud.

With a panicked pace to my heart, I knew there was no way I could prepare the messages without His help, so the only option was to talk about what He wanted to talk about. As quickly as I could.

So I got down on my knees and listened. Five days later, God was still talking. About sin! In my life! Every time I opened my Bible, a verse seemed to leap up off the page, indicting me for another sin I hadn't been aware of. It was awful. Painful. Humiliating.

This dialogue with a very holy God was triggered by a little book I was reading by another old-timey revivalist.[1] The third chapter was titled, "Preparing the

Heart for Revival." He based his comments on Hosea 10:12: "Break up your unplowed ground; for it is time to seek the LORD, until he comes and showers righteousness on you."

The author explained that, to experience revival, we must look to our hearts and the spiritual ground that has perhaps become hardened over time and—like Daddy Graham and his cornfield—plow it up. We must examine the state of our minds. Reflect on our past actions.

The revivalist cautioned that he did not mean we were to glance at things, and then make a general confession to God *for all our sins* the way many of us do. He challenged the reader to take pen and paper and write down each sin as it came to mind. Because our sins are committed one at a time, he said they must be reviewed and repented of one by one. To get the reader started, he included a list of sins that I have reworded slightly, but you will still get the point. Among those sins:

Ingratitude. List all the favors God has bestowed, before and after salvation. Which ones have I forgotten to thank Him for?

Losing Love for God. Consider how devastated I would be if my husband or children not only were lessened in their love for me, but increasingly loved someone or something else more. Is there evidence I've been lessening in my love for Him?

Neglect of Bible Reading. Has my daily Bible reading been pushed aside by an over-full schedule; or, as I read my Bible, am I constantly preoccupied with other things? How long has it been since reading my Bible was a delight? Do I read it so casually that I don't even remember what it says when I'm finished?

Unbelief. Refusing to believe or to expect that He will give me what He has promised is to accuse Him of lying. What promise have I thought He would not give me? What prayer did I think He would not answer?

Neglect of Prayer. I will put this one in my own words. Prayers are not spiritual chatter, offered without fervent, focused faith. Have I substituted wishing, daydreaming, or fantasizing for real prayer?

Lack of Concern for the Souls of Others. Standing by and watching friends, neighbors, coworkers, and even family members on their way to hell, yet not caring enough to warn them or pray for them or even admit that's where they will end up if they don't put their faith in Jesus. Have I become so politically correct that I don't apply the Gospel to those I know and love?

Neglect of Family. Putting myself and my needs before them. What effort have I made, what habit have I established, for my family's spiritual good?

This list is painful, isn't it? But the revivalist wasn't finished. He kept going.

Love of the World and Material Things. Assess what I own. Do I think my possessions are mine? That my money is mine? That I can spend it as I choose?

Pride. Vanity about my appearance. More time spent in getting ready for church than preparing my heart and mind to worship when I get there. Am I offended, or even slightly irritated, if others don't notice my appearance?

Envy. Jealousy of those who seem more fruitful or gifted or recognizable than I am. Do I struggle with hearing others praised?

A Critical Spirit. God has given me a spirit of discernment. But do I use it to find fault with others who don't measure up to my standards?

Slander. Telling the truth with the intention of causing people to think less of a person. Whose faults, real or imagined, have I discussed behind their backs? Why have I?

Lack of Seriousness toward God. Showing disrespect for God as though He doesn't really matter. Do I give Him the leftovers of my emotions, time, thoughts, money?

Lying. Designed deception. Anything that is contrary to the unvarnished truth. What have I said that was designed to impress someone, but it wasn't the whole truth? Or was an exaggeration of the truth?

Cheating. Treating others in a way I wouldn't want to be treated myself. Have I stopped short of treating others with the same regard?

Hypocrisy. Am I pretending to be anything I am not?

Temper. Losing patience with a child, coworker, friend, spouse, or staff member. What cross words have I spoken lately?

Arrogance. Have I accepted God's forgiveness while refusing to forgive myself or someone else?

That's quite a list! The original author gave instructions that after the reader had carefully considered each of these sins, he or she was to go back and reread the list, writing down any other sins that come to mind. When that exercise was completed, he said to do it again. A third time.

CONFESSION OF PERSONAL SHAME

To humor this old man who is now in glory, I followed his instructions. The first time I went down the list, I finished with gratitude that not one of the sins described me! After a second reading, I thought that if I stretched the meaning of some of the sins he listed, I could see the slight possibility of a few of them in my life.

Feeling very spiritual for being honest enough to glimpse traces of sin in my own heart, I read the list for the third time. And that's when I was laid bare. God used that list of sins to shine the light of His Truth deep down into the dark inner recesses of my heart. It was like having a spiritual angiogram. The sins revealed went farther and broader than just those on the list. Altogether, my time of conviction, confession, and cleansing lasted for seven days! And I was in ministry! Deeply involved in prayer and in studying, applying, and living out God's Word to the best of my ability! Committed to sharing His Word with others!

How could I have allowed the sin to pile up like that in my heart and life? I was deeply ashamed before God. And still am.

In fact, I think one reason some of us, myself included, don't examine our hearts for sin is because we are so afraid we will find it. One thing I've discovered is that it takes courage to look deep within to see what God sees. It's painful to acknowledge that we're not as righteous, pure, or holy as we thought we were.

It's even more shameful to acknowledge that, with my family background and with all the time I spent in God's Word and in prayer, I should have known better. But like cobwebs in the corners of a dusty, unkempt attic, my heart had held unconfessed sin. So for seven days I clung to the old rugged Cross. I discovered in a fresh, very personal way that the blood of Jesus is not just for unsaved sinners who come to the Cross for the first time, but for saved sinners who need to come back and back and back. Praise God! The blood of Jesus never runs out. It never loses its power to cleanse and to wash us as white as snow.

Three days before my seminar was to begin, God indicated that He was finished convicting and cleansing. At least for that time. When I asked Him, *Are You sure? I don't want to miss anything,* He gave me a sweet, blessed assurance that I was cleansed of my sin and my shame and filled with His Spirit. When I once again picked up my pad and pencil to work on the messages, my thoughts flowed freely. By the time the seminar began, I was prepared.

Looking back, I now know that what I experienced was revival. Personal revival. It's what I have longed to see take place corporately so that the entire church and our nation are restored. Which leads me back to Daniel's prayer. I am convinced that the key to revival is repentance. And that the key to repentance is prayer. Not prayer that preaches at people, but prayer that is offered with wet eyes, a broken heart, and bent knees.

There was nothing judgmental or self-righteous in Daniel's words. He prayed with a conscious awareness of his own sin as he prayed for the sin he saw in others. I believe it's a lesson that must be learned if our prayers are going to claim the promises of God. So . . . before we apply Daniel's prayer to the sins of others, would you take a moment to search your own heart? Then confess your sins. Tell God you are sorry. Ask Him to cleanse you. Of all of them.

Take as long as you need. Seven minutes, seven hours, seven days, seven weeks, seven months. Just do it. Plow up the fallow ground of your heart so He can send you showers of His blessing and righteousness. Draw a circle around yourself and make sure that everything in it is right with God . . . as He sees you. As you pray for revival, ask Him to let it begin with you.

Once our hearts are broken for our own sin, then we are ready to intercede with God for the sins of others.

CONFESSION OF SHAME
FOR THE CHURCH

Even within churches, we can see a moral "twilight" and encroaching darkness. Entire denominations have turned off the light by denying that Jesus is the only way to God . . . the Bible is God's infallible, inerrant, inspired Word . . . there is a hell and there is a Heaven . . . and the list could go on. Sin is either rationalized, denied, or covered up.

This was brought home to me not too long ago, when I was invited to speak in a fast-growing mega-church led by a dynamic young pastor. The pastor had given me the freedom to speak on any subject I chose. I felt God lead me to present the Gospel as clearly and as winsomely as I could. So at each of the multiple Sunday-morning worship services, that's just what I did. However, the congregation did not seem responsive, and the reason emerged from the pastor's response at the conclusion of the morning. With a grim tone, he remarked, "Anne, we don't talk about judgment here."

His comment caught me up short as thoughts swirled in my head: *Is that why his church is growing so fast? Is that why he's so popular? When God's Word is unpleasant, uncomfortable, is it also unspoken?*

Church leaders can give the impression that they

have a greater desire to have large congregations, to be accepted and successful, to be published authors or radio personalities or conference speakers than to hold up the Truth. They seem to care more about their own reputations and favorable public opinion than God's opinion.

It's shameful.

I'll never forget my conversation with a man who had been a religion editor for a major newspaper. He said he had placed his faith in Jesus as his Savior. He had joined a Bible study, made Christian friends, and attended church. But within a few years, he became convinced that he'd been deceived. He ended up totally rejecting Jesus and becoming an outspoken agnostic. The reason? The hypocrisy he saw within the church.

He went so far in the conversation as to name specifics, then concluded in words something like this: "Anne, I have seen no difference in the behavior of those inside the church than with those outside the church. It's just that outside the church we don't pretend to be righteous." I honestly wish I could have said I didn't know what he was talking about. But I did.

If a church leader is exposed as an adulterer, he may be removed, but then his behavior is excused as an addiction, and he gains acceptance with another congregation. If an individual believer is wealthy and powerful, his sin is quickly rationalized and the person is catered to because of his philanthropy. Couples living in sin are given the blessing of the church.

It's shameful.

It's also dangerous. When the church either dims the light of God's Truth, or turns the Light off altogether, the nation begins operating and functioning in spiritual darkness. There is no guiding light to show the nation how to get back on the right path.

In North Carolina, our rugged coast has been nicknamed the Graveyard of the Atlantic because so many ships have come to ruin on our treacherous Outer Banks. So our shoreline remains dotted with lighthouses. The purpose of each one is to help ships find their way safely in the dark. Without them, ships have to guess their way through dangerous waters and currents.[2]

The church in many real ways is intended to be the spiritual lighthouse of a nation, warning when a nation veers from a safe course. It is a guiding light that shows a nation how to return to the right path. But if the light has grown dim through compromise or turned off altogether, then the nation increasingly founders in the stormy seas of moral and spiritual relativism.

The sinful, shameful condition of our nation today and the church within her borders is not only scorned in Heaven, but brings scorn to the name of God on earth.

Personal Confession
for Global Scorn

I wonder if Judah's sin and shame had so gripped Daniel's heart that, with a voice choking in emotion, he blurted out what he felt was the worst consequence of all: "Our sins and . . . iniquities . . . have made . . . your people an object of scorn to all those around us" (9:16).

The nations of the world looked at God's people and saw them in captivity—their cities devastated, their temple destroyed. If Judah's God was anywhere around, there was no evidence of His power or protection. Which led the nations to conclude that her God was not God after all. Or if He was God, He was not supreme and could be conquered and rendered impotent by others. And so His Name was held in derision.

Rather than exclusively applying this to our nation, which seems to no longer be identified as Christian, it may be clearer to see the parallel with the church and with individual believers. Because every time a church leader is caught in sexual immorality . . . every time a Christian is caught lying or cheating . . . every time a crime is committed by a church deacon or elder . . . it is *God's Name* that is derided.

Our sinful behavior makes a mockery of who He is to the world around us. Instead of looking at us and seeing a reflection of Jesus, the world looks at us and sees a reflection of themselves. We are perceived as practical atheists who say we believe in God but act as though He doesn't exist. Which leads the world to dismiss Him as irrelevant.

So, as you and I plow up the fallow ground of our hearts, we would do well to ask ourselves some searching questions:

Who has rejected God because of my behavior or conversation?

Am I driving people away from Him or drawing them to Him by my behavior and attitude?

Does the Light in my life shine so that others look at my character and my conduct and genuinely praise the One who lives within me?

Or is the Light so dim that they don't notice any difference between myself and them?

If you and I want to storm the gates of Heaven and ignite a raging fire of revival in our nation, then Daniel's example makes it clear that we must begin with wet eyes, bent knees, and a broken heart . . . for our own sin.

CHAPTER 6

PLEADING WITH CLARITY

S ometimes my prayers remind me of looking
through a pair of binoculars. Occasionally when
I've begun to pray, my vision seems blurred. As though
my prayer is fuzzy because I don't know exactly what to
pray for or how to pray. But like adjusting the focus on
the binoculars while I look through them, I've found
that my thoughts become clearer and my requests more
specific as I pray.

Daniel must have experienced something similar because he alludes to the fact that God gave him

insight and understanding "while I was still in prayer" (9:21). I find this encouraging. We don't have to have a clear comprehension of the need or the solution. We don't have to tell God how to "fix" things or even suggest a course of action. What a relief that all we have to do is to get down on our knees and state the problem! The burden to resolve the situation is His, not yours and mine.

SIMPLICITY IN PRAYER

In addition to praying when we don't know the answers, we are also free to pray without using eloquent speech or poetic phrases. The simplicity of just stating the need is beautifully illustrated by Jesus's own mother, Mary, during a wedding reception in Cana of Galilee. The celebration almost ended prematurely when the wine ran out before the festivities had concluded.

While the crisis doesn't seem catastrophic to us, it would have been so to the bride and groom in that day. To run out of wine was considered the height of rudeness, indicating a lack of hospitality due to inadequate preparation. It could have led to the bridegroom being sued by the bride's family. At the very least, the young couple would have been humiliated in the eyes of their family, friends, and neighbors. This is definitely not the way most couples want to begin their life together.[1]

Mary did not hyperventilate in panic or try to fix the situation herself. She just went to Jesus, who was in attendance, and stated the problem, "They have no more wine."[2] What could have been simpler? As His mother, she could have been tempted to tell Him what to do and how to do it. But she didn't even make a suggestion. She just stated the need.

She centered her "prayer" on Jesus because she believed . . . *she knew* . . . He was not only her son, but God's Son. And she knew Him well enough to know that He would care about the crisis and do something about it.

In response to His mother's simple statement, He performed the first miracle of His ministry. He turned water into wine, and the crisis was averted.

We can learn much from Mary's example here. Too often when we pray, we seem to forget that God already knows the details of our requests and how to respond in His infinite wisdom. Perhaps, like me, you've heard prayers similar to this one:

Dear God,
My cousin's mother, that's my father's brother's wife, needs your help. She's seventy years old and has really bad arthritis. The other day she was working in her vegetable garden—even at her age she still loves working outdoors—when she stumbled and fell and broke her hip. Her right one. She lay there until her neighbor spotted her and called 911. Thank You,

Lord, for letting her neighbor find her. So she's going to need surgery to replace her hip. Please heal her and give her doctor wisdom about how to operate . . . and also . . . and finally . . . Amen.

Forgive me for exaggerating, but haven't we all heard prayers like this one? Maybe even prayed this way ourselves? It seems humorous when we stop to think about it, but it also reveals a superficial understanding of who God is. God is God! He can do anything and He knows everything. All you and I need to do is place our burdens in His capable hands. Crawl up in His lap, put your head on His shoulder, and rest in Him. Sometimes no words are necessary. Weep if you must. He can interpret the tears.

INTENSITY IN PRAYER

As Daniel continued to pour out his heart, his prayer came more clearly into focus. With almost rapid-fire intensity, he stated what he was pleading for: "Turn away your anger and your wrath from Jerusalem, your city, your holy hill. . . . Hear the prayers and petitions of your servant. . . . Look with favor on your desolate sanctuary. Give ear, our God, and hear; open your eyes and see. . . . Lord, listen! Lord, forgive! Lord, hear and act!" (9:16–19).

While Daniel doesn't refer to a specific passage of God's Word here, his prayer reflected a promise given hundreds of years earlier. When King Solomon had dedicated the temple, God vowed to hear prayers offered for Jerusalem.[3] He promised to look on the city He loved and to always care for it.

Daniel's entire prayer became intensely focused on asking God for what He wanted to give and what He had promised to give. His example teaches us to pray until we enter into the very heart of the Father. We discover His "wants" through the promises in His Word, which the Holy Spirit will impress on our hearts.

DISCOVERY IN PRAYER

We need to pray until we can unload all we are thinking and all we want in order to get down to what God is thinking and what He wants. Then we ask Him for what we know He wants to give us. A good example is the prayer Abraham prayed for Sodom.

Abraham felt burdened for the spiritual condition of the world around him, for the city closest to him, and for his own family members that he knew were in danger of coming under judgment. His burden came straight from the heart of God. And how did he know the heart of God? He had spent time walking with God.

In some respects, walking with God is similar to

walking with each other. Every morning that I'm home, I get up early and walk around a lake in a nearby park. I sometimes walk with a friend, not only for safety, but for the fellowship. Two basic rules stay the same, regardless of who walks with me: we must walk in the same direction, and we must walk at the same pace. If either of those rules is not kept, then it doesn't matter how much I enjoy the other person, or how committed we are to our friendship, we won't be walking together.

Likewise, if we want to walk with God, we must walk in His direction, which means surrendering the will of our lives to Him. We can't go off in our own direction, deciding our own goals and pursuing our own purposes. And we must walk at His pace, which means step-by-step obedience to His Word. Since we have no idea what steps He is taking on a particular day, we have to read and apply His Word on a daily basis so that we can adjust our pace to His.

As Abraham walked with God, God revealed that He was going to destroy Sodom and Gomorrah.[4] And so Abraham began to pray for what he knew was on God's mind and heart: the people who were living in Sodom. His prayer revealed that he didn't know exactly what to ask for, so he started by asking God to spare Sodom for the sake of fifty righteous people who lived there. When God agreed, Abraham's prayer progressed to asking for Sodom to be spared for forty people, then thirty, then twenty, then ten people.

Each request Abraham made was answered by God in agreement. But after God agreed to spare Sodom for the sake of ten righteous people who lived there, God finished speaking with Abraham and then left. Abraham never voiced what I think must have been the deepest prayer of his heart, which was for his nephew Lot to be saved from judgment when it fell. But God knew.

It's encouraging to me to know I don't have to always say things exactly right when I pray. I just need to pray. And God, who searches my heart and knows the deep desires that are there, will answer in His own way.[5]

God knew the real desire in Abraham's heart. When He couldn't even find ten righteous people living in Sodom, He destroyed it . . . yet remembering Abraham's prayer, God supernaturally delivered Lot and his family from His judgment.[6] Lot's salvation is what Abraham had undoubtedly wanted. And that's what God had wanted to give him when He first imparted His burden to Abraham, moving him to pray accordingly.

SENSITIVITY IN PRAYER

Jesus promised His disciples that the Holy Spirit would guide them into all truth, bringing to their minds the things they needed to remember.[7] While He was certainly speaking of the anointing His disciples were given in order to record His words in the New Testament writings . . . while He certainly was reassuring them that when they were placed on trial for their faith, they could rely on the Holy Spirit to give them answers for their interrogators . . . I also believe that what He said can be applied to our prayers for our families, our churches, our nation, and our world. In other words, one application of what Jesus promised was that as we pray, God the Holy Spirit would bring to our minds the Scripture on which we need to base our prayers. But the Holy Spirit can't bring to our remembrance things we have never known or read. This is one reason it's so important to saturate ourselves in Scripture.

One time a friend texted me for prayer when her husband was recuperating from open-heart surgery. As I prayed, Psalm 73:26 came to mind, which promises, "My flesh and my heart may fail, but God is the strength of my heart and my portion forever." So I claimed that promise in prayer for her husband. Within the week, he was released from the hospital to continue his recovery at home.

When you pray, ask the Holy Spirit to teach you how to pray. And what to pray. Take your Bible into your place of prayer. As you read it, open your heart and mind to His still, small voice that whispers in your "ear" and gives direction to your thoughts and words.[8] In prayer, be sensitive to Him.

Priority in Prayer

~

The last words recorded in Daniel's prayer are, "Lord, listen! Lord, forgive! Lord, hear and act!" *Why? What was the basic reason for his entire prayer?* "For your sake, my God, do not delay, because your city and your people bear your Name" (9:19). There it is, like a nugget of gold gleaming in the stream of his prayer!

Having pleaded with confidence in God's character and in God's covenant; having acknowledged that his people had spurned repeated warnings and therefore deserved the judgment they had received; having pleaded with fasting, in sackcloth and ashes, in honest and humble confession of sin and shame and scorn; having voiced his desperation for God to make good on His promise given through Jeremiah to set his people free after seventy years of captivity, Daniel stated very simply and succinctly what his prayer was all about. It was a heartfelt plea for God to be glorified in His city and in His people for His own great Name's sake. His entire prayer became focused on asking God for what He wanted to give.

And therein lies the secret to the prayer that storms Heaven's gates. Bottom line, Daniel's priority in prayer was that God's Name be cleared. Exalted. That the shame brought to it by the behavior of His people and their subsequent judgment would be cleansed as God kept His promise to release them from captivity and restore them to His place of blessing. Daniel longed for the nations of the world to recognize that Israel's God is God. He longed for the world to acknowledge that his God is indeed faithful and gracious and good and great.

As you pray, what is your heartfelt priority?

Relief from pain?

Reconciliation of a relationship?

Restoration of health?

Resolution of financial issues?

Recognition of your profile?

Reinstatement to your job?

Removal of an enemy?

Repression of gossip?

Rescue from trouble?

Reward for well-doing?

I've prayed for all of the above, and more. But while I'm free to pour out my heart and tell God what I want, overarching them all is the priority of God's glory. I long for God's Name to be exalted through the way my prayer is, *or is not*, answered.

PART 3

PREVAILING
IN PRAYER

*I have heard the prayer and plea
you have made before me.*
1 Kings 9:3

CHAPTER 7

ANSWERED
IMMEDIATELY

Once I articulate what I'm asking God for, once I have Scripture to confirm that what I am asking Him to give me is what He also wants me to receive, once I'm confident He has heard my prayer, I don't have to keep begging. I know He knows. And how do I know He has heard and will answer? Because the burden in my heart will lift. I will feel released from it. Then I transition into waiting mode. Even as I pray about other things or get on to the business of my day, my spirit remains in a position of waiting, anticipating His answer.

Throughout history, God has honored the prevailing

prayers of His people. Elijah had victoriously challenged the wicked, idolatrous priests of Baal to a contest
that revealed once and for all to the people whose god
was God. But Elijah's work was not done. God had
promised him that if he would confront the wicked
King Ahab and the priests of Baal, then God would
end the three-year drought Israel was experiencing.
So Elijah climbed back up on Mt. Carmel, crouched
down with his face to the ground, and prayed for rain.
It didn't come. So he prayed again. It didn't come. He
prayed again. And again. And again. And again. And
again—seven times! Finally a small cloud was spotted
that signaled God's answer. Before Elijah could get to
cover, the rain began to pour down.[1] Elijah had prevailed in prayer.

Hundreds of years before Elijah, Abraham's grand-
son Jacob was returning to Canaan after twenty years
in exile. His intention was to claim the birthright that
he had bought from his brother, Esau, and stolen from
his father, Isaac. When he came to the border of the
land promised to him (marked by the Jabbok River), he
sent his family, his livestock, and his servants on ahead
of him.

It was evening when he stepped out to follow them.
But his way was blocked by a Man who would not let
him pass. Jacob then wrestled with the Man all night,
refusing to give in or give up. Finally the Man broke
Jacob's hip. But instead of crumbling at the Man's feet

and whimpering in self-pity, Jacob wound his arms around the Man's neck and said he would not let go until the Man blessed him. And who was the Man? He was none other than the Lord God.[2] Jacob had prevailed in prayer.

What does it mean to prevail in prayer? On the one hand, if we keep repeating the same prayer over and over, it implies we lack the faith to believe God has heard and will answer. On the other hand, having prayed once, we can't just walk away until it's answered. We need to pray like Elijah—praying repeatedly until we have the assurance God has heard and will answer— then we thank Him by faith for the answer even before it comes, and rise up from our knees.

Simply put, prevailing prayer means to persevere until you receive the answer. It means to stay on your face and refuse to settle for less than everything God has promised. It means to put your arms of faith about your Father's neck and cling tightly to Him until He blesses you. But you must be sure that what you are praying for is something God wants to give you. You base your prayer on God's Word. Then your spirit holds a position of prayer before God until an answer is given.

Daniel didn't have to wait long. He had pleaded with laser-focused confidence, heartrending confession, and pinpoint clarity. And before he finished praying, an answer came by special delivery: "[The angel] Gabriel . . . instructed me and said to me, '. . . As soon as you began to pray, a word [an answer] went out, which I have come to tell you . . .'" (9:21–23).

The incredible revelation was that Heaven was moved as soon as Daniel began to pray! God didn't wait to see how long Daniel would hold out in his fasting or leave the ashes smeared on his face. The prayer that is heard by Heaven is not a legalistic exercise where you and I prove to God we are somehow spiritual enough, worthy enough, humble enough, desperate enough, sincere enough to earn an answer. God looks on the heart of the one who is praying. He is moved by our trust in Him. In Him alone.

He is not an "add-on" God. As we pray, we cannot have several options up our sleeve. Daniel's prayer was wholly and exclusively centered on God. We pray absolutely convinced that if God does not come through for us, we won't come through. That if He doesn't help us, we won't be helped. If He doesn't save us, we're doomed. But for those who put their trust in Him alone, they discover He is the God of the impossible who finds great delight in making a way where there is no way.

Immediately Encouraged by the Answer

He is a God of miracles who also loves to encourage us in prayer.

How wonderful would it be if, as we were praying, an angel would show up with the answer! That has never happened to me. But I have received answers to prayer from God's appointed "messengers."

One messenger stands out in my mind because the answer he gave was a dramatic turning point for me during a very difficult time. Several years ago in my ministry, I uncovered a full-time staff person who was simultaneously working on another job. When I confronted her with it, she irately accused me of lying, insisted she was entitled to supplement her income, and appealed over my head to the ministry's board of directors. After hearing her thoroughly state her case, the board unanimously recommended that she be terminated. Which she was. Although she had entered into a signed covenant with the other two ministry directors, when she left they pledged to stay. However, two weeks after her termination, they both turned in their resignations.

Suddenly I was left with a ministry that was facing four major national and international initiatives within the next nine months, but without the directors who would have helped me accomplish them. To say I prayed is an understatement. I was launched into that stratosphere of faith where I was wholly centered on God and God alone, knowing beyond a shadow of a doubt that if He did not help me, my ministry would collapse.

Within twenty-four hours God sent His messenger to me, the husband of one of my board members. I was attending a meeting that just "happened" to have been scheduled for the day after I had learned of the mass exodus of directors from my ministry. This board member and her husband, Vicki and Ray Bentley, were among others at the meeting. The three of us had just finished discussing my situation when we walked from lunch to the next conference seminar.

As we walked through the hotel corridor, they told me they had just been to Mount Vernon, the historic estate of President Washington. I thought, *What does that have to do with the situation I'm in?* but I listened. Ray went on to say that one thing he had learned was that Washington should never have won the Revolutionary War. But he *did* win because God had brought him great generals who helped him. Then Ray stopped me, put his hands on my shoulders so that I had to look him directly in the eye, and delivered the initial answer to my prayer: "Anne, God will bring you generals."

Deep in my heart, the burden was lifted. *I knew* God had heard my prayer and would bring me through. I assure you that I maintained a position of prayer in my heart while I continued to wait for the specific answers, but God's peace flooded my heart and never left. I was greatly encouraged that God had heard my prayer.

Immediately Encouraged
by the Affirmation

The very fact that Gabriel had been sent by God to give Daniel a message must have immediately relieved the burden that weighed so heavily on Daniel's heart. Until that moment, Daniel would not have known for sure if he had interpreted Jeremiah's prophecy accurately . . . if he had been praying appropriately . . . if anyone was listening or moving in response to his prayer.

Gabriel's message also affirmed Daniel personally when the angel revealed, "Daniel . . . you are highly esteemed" (9:22–23). What an amazing revelation for an old man, isolated in an upstairs room, enslaved in a foreign land, who had been pouring out his heart as he interceded for his nation and his people!

This affirmation is something for you and me to wrap our hearts and minds around. If there was no other reward for prayer than earning Heaven's high regard, wouldn't that be enough? When everything is said and done, nothing else really matters, does it?

If you enter into prayer as Daniel did, you will be highly esteemed by God. That's more than encouraging! That's exhilarating! It makes all of the fasting and ashes and rags and hours spent on your knees worth it a hundred times over! God will also bring into your life visible people who will affirm you and bless you.

Immediately Enlightened

Gabriel additionally revealed to Daniel, "I have now come to give you insight and understanding" (9:22). Prayer is almost like a flower that begins as a tightly closed bud but then blossoms into fullness as we pray.

Sometimes my prayers are tightly closed at first because I am in a panic mode. Desperation causes me to see only one way to pray, and it usually is something like, "Get me out of this! Deliver me!" But as I settle down in my spirit, as I deliberately calm myself and choose to obey God's scriptural command not to be afraid, my spiritual fingers relax around my tightly clasped demand and I begin to let go of what I think I have to have and when I have to have it.

Four weeks before I was supposed to lead a citywide revival a few years back, the doctor informed me that I needed to have emergency abdominal surgery for diverticulitis. He assured me I would be strong enough in a month's time to lead the revival. I felt I had no choice but to comply, and the discovery that my colon had been abscessed confirmed I had made the right choice. But my recovery was complicated by a severe case of vertigo. I could barely stand without weaving because of the disorientation caused by the dizziness. So with the vertigo added to the physical pain and weakness from the surgery, panic set in. That's when I began to demand that God do something. Now. Or at least do something by the time I left home to go to the city of the revival. But all I "heard" in response was silence.

I reminded God, as though He had forgotten, that the platform I used in our revivals was a round platform anchored by a podium in the shape of an old wooden cross. Once I was on it, there would be no place to hide—nothing to sit down on and nothing to cling to. I was so convinced I was going to collapse on the platform that I instructed Fernando Ortega, who led worship at the revivals, to be prepared with a few appropriate songs to cover the awkwardness when I did collapse.

As I continued to desperately pray and nothing happened, I could "feel" my spiritual fingers losing their grip on my demand. Finally, I let go. I told the Lord if my collapse would in some way bring Him glory, if He wanted to use a public display of my weakness to break through and break down the barriers so that real revival would take place, I *was* willing for that to happen. And I *was* willing, even though I was filled with dread.

The next morning, after I surrendered my demand for miraculous healing and deliverance, God "enlightened" me. I was sitting at my computer, with my Bible open as I worked on the notes for one of the messages, when my eye fell on Psalm 46:5 . . . "God is within her, she will not fall; God will help her at break of day." That verse pulsated with life! To this day, it still reverberates with the sound of His voice.

Immediately I received enormous release from the burden I had been carrying. The very next morning, as I opened one of my devotional books during my prayer time, Psalm 121:3 seemed to leap up off the page, confirming what He had said the day before: "He will not let your foot slip . . ." The promise was emphatic. I began to praise God for the strength I knew He would give to get me through my responsibilities, not just somehow, but triumphantly.

While I certainly realize the danger of taking God's Word out of context, I also know my Shepherd's voice. After six decades of following Him, I know by experience that when I read my Bible, God speaks to me personally and specifically. I've learned how to listen when He speaks to my spirit. I also know this by faith. God's Word clearly testifies about itself that "all Scripture is God-breathed and is useful for teaching, rebuking, correcting, and training in righteousness, so that the servant of God may be thoroughly equipped for every good work."[3]

As the time drew nearer for me to climb up on the platform, I began to get apprehensive once again. Although I was healing nicely from the surgery, my vertigo was in full force. I can't recall how I was led to Psalm 61:2, but I know I used it to voice my fear . . . "Lord, I call as my heart grows faint; lead me to the rock that is higher than I." Once again, He immediately gave me enlightenment from Psalm 40:2, "Anne,

[I] will set [your] feet on a rock and give [you] a firm place to stand. [I] will put a new song in [your] mouth, a hymn of praise to our God. Many will see and fear and put their trust in the LORD."

As I stepped up on the platform that Friday for the evening session, and again on Saturday morning for multiple sessions that would last until 5:00 that afternoon, God was true to His Word. My foot did not slip, nor did I collapse.

I will be the first to acknowledge that not all prayers are answered immediately with encouragement and enlightenment. When the answer is delayed, I can get discouraged and give up instead of prevailing in prayer. Which makes me wonder what answers, blessings, and miracles I have missed because I gave up after the sixth time of interceding? Or because, when God seemingly refused to give in to my demand, my faith collapsed and I didn't hang on until He blessed me?

That's why I have resolved to keep storming the gates of Heaven until I receive what He has promised. Would you share this same resolve? Drive the stake of your faith deep down into His promise. Don't give up. Don't give in. Don't collapse. Don't settle for less than prayer that claims the promises of God and moves Heaven.

CHAPTER 8

ANSWERED ULTIMATELY

We know Daniel never forgot his boyhood experience of growing up in Jerusalem, indicated by the fact that when he prayed he always opened his windows toward his beloved city. But he also would have known of the devastation caused by King Nebuchadnezzar and the Babylonian army following his capture. Not only had the city of Jerusalem been destroyed, but the temple itself had been leveled so that nothing remained. The bronze, the gold, the treasures, the artifacts—all were seized. Taken to Babylon. No one who loved and worshiped God in the temple would ever forget.

Daniel had seen with his own eyes the sacred golden vessels of temple worship being used at a pagan feast for the pleasure of a spoiled, drunken Babylonian king.[1] He knew the city of Jerusalem was nothing but ruins and the temple a pile of rubble. No tendril of smoke had lifted for forty-seven years because, without the temple, there had been no more sacrifices.[2]

As Daniel prayed, he must have been gazing out of his upstairs window, visualizing the city he had once known. We know from his prayer that his heart was filled with longing for the day when the temple would be rebuilt. The sacrifices would be reinstituted. The streets of Jerusalem would once again be filled with throngs of people going up to the House of the Lord with songs on their lips and a spotless lamb in tow. His heart must have almost exploded with desire for the nations of the world once again to stand in awe of Israel's God.

These thoughts must have been on Daniel's mind, because God answered in a very subtle yet symbolic way. Daniel clearly remembered, "While I was speaking and praying, confessing my sin and the sin of my people Israel and making my request to the LORD my God for his holy hill—while I was still in prayer, Gabriel, the man I had seen in the earlier vision, came to me in swift flight *about the time of the evening sacrifice*" (9:20–21, emphasis mine). That was an unmistakable message. God is not whimsical, nor does He act randomly. He is very purposeful not only in what He says but in the way He says it and when He says it.

So . . . why did God's answer to Daniel's prayer come at the time of the evening sacrifice? Could it be that God was revealing a mystery? That the ultimate answer to all of the above would take place about five hundred years later? Around three o'clock in the afternoon, at the time of the evening sacrifice? On the Holy Hill of Calvary as the spotless Lamb of God was slain as a sacrifice for the sin of the world?

I want to be careful not to put words in God's mouth, but is it possible that God was conveying something like the following?

Daniel, I've heard and will answer your prayer. I will set your people free. They will go home. Jerusalem and the temple will be rebuilt. But beloved Daniel, there is much more. The city of Jerusalem and its temple are just replicas. They are shadows of a Heavenly Home where one day I will dwell with My people forever.[3] And the sacrifices are just audio-visual aids that point to My Lamb. One day, I will send My own Son as the Lamb who will die for the sin of the world.[4] And forever after, anyone and everyone who places their faith in Him will be forgiven of their sin,

cleansed of their guilt, and saved from My judgment. One day, Daniel, they will truly be free at
last! Free once and for all from sin's penalty and
sin's power. One day My Son will open the gates
of Heaven, and all those who trust in Him will
live forever with Me in the New Jerusalem.[5] They
will all go Home! O Daniel, there is an ultimate
answer to your prayer, and His Name is Jesus!

I am convinced that the ultimate answer to Daniel's
prayer today is still Jesus. Because people are still being
held captive—not necessarily by conquering nations
(although some surely are), but by the real enemy of our
souls, the devil. The devil has bound them in chains
of sin and selfishness and lust and greed. The enslave-
ment of men and women of every age, nationality,
language, and culture is why I am compelled to pray
that all people everywhere would be saved and come to
a knowledge of the truth.[6]

And make no mistake about it. The truth is Jesus,
the Liberator of our souls and the Terminator of our
enemy.[7] Our prayers move Heaven and earth as one
person at a time fully embraces Jesus as the Ultimate
Answer . . .

One person like the apostle Paul who testified,
"Christ Jesus came into the world to save sinners—of
whom I am the worst. But for that very reason I was
shown mercy so that in me, the worst of sinners,

Christ Jesus might display his unlimited patience as an example for those who would believe on him and receive eternal life."[8] Paul went on to turn the entire world of his day upside down as he proclaimed the Ultimate Answer through his preaching, as well as through his writing, which comprises much of the New Testament.[9] In a little more than three hundred years after Paul, the Gospel had so permeated the known world that Christianity was adopted as the official religion of the Roman Empire.

One person like William Carey (1761–1834), a cobbler who heard God's call to the nations in the quietness of his shoe shop. It is said that he burst into tears and responded with the words of Isaiah, "Here am I; send me."[10] Considered the greatest missionary of the modern world, he proclaimed the Gospel in India for forty-one years, translated and published the Scriptures into forty different languages, and successfully worked to ban *sati*, the practice of burning widows alive when their husbands died. One of his sermon titles seems to summarize his life of service: "Expect great things from God. Attempt great things for God."[11]

One person like Hudson Taylor (1832–1905). As a young man he forsook the faith of his parents but, at the age of seventeen, embraced Jesus as his personal Lord and Savior. As a British missionary, he founded the China Inland Mission to proclaim the Ultimate Answer for fifty-one years in every province of China.

Today, the Chinese church is one of the largest, fastest-growing churches in the world.

One person like C. T. Studd (1860–1931), the wealthy, privileged young man who became a nationally recognized cricket player and captain of his team at Eton College in England. Born again at the age of eighteen, he was living proof of what it means to embrace Jesus without looking back. He is remembered as saying, "Some wish to live within the sound of Church or Chapel bell; I want to run a Rescue Shop within a yard of hell." And so he did. Heaven was moved and nations were changed as he proclaimed Christ to China, India, and the heart of Africa.[12]

One person like Jim Elliot (1927–1956), who embraced Jesus at the tender age of six. He was raised by parents who were devoted to the Gospel and who encouraged him to be adventurous as he lived for Christ. As a young adult, he felt called to share the Ultimate Answer to the Quechua Indians of Ecuador. While working with them, he heard of an unreached, violent group whose name means "savage"—the Auca Indians. He and four other missionaries made contact with the Aucas.

After receiving encouraging responses to their overtures, the five missionaries landed their small plane along the Curaray River, where they established a base. But in spite of the seeming friendliness of the Aucas, all five young men were speared to death. Even though

Jim Elliot's life was brief, it demonstrated his core belief as expressed in his most well-known quote, "He is no fool who gives what he cannot keep to gain that which he cannot lose."

Jim Elliot's powerful witness resounded around the world when he was featured in a *Life* magazine cover story shortly after his death. His wife, Elisabeth Elliot, a well-known author and speaker herself, continued his legacy through two biographies—*Shadow of the Almighty* and *Through Gates of Splendor*—challenging a new generation to take the Gospel to the uttermost parts of the earth. And in 2006 a movie was released, *End of the Spear*, that chronicled the successful, continuing effort to reach the natives of Ecuador.

One person like Azzam, a former pirate somewhere in Somalia today, who rides back and forth between countries in coffins, under corpses, to deliver the precious cargo of God's Word because he knows Somali Muslims will not open a casket or touch a dead body.

How could he have ever come to the decision to engage in such a mission? Azzam was born and raised a Muslim but kept having dreams of Jesus. He sought out his Imam for answers, but the man violently berated and beat him. When Azzam's mother discovered he was having Jesus dreams, she commanded him to leave the home for his own protection and never come back. He did.

Though he walked miles and miles, his father—a powerful warlord—located him quickly and sent

Azzam a package. When Azzam opened it, he was sickened to find his mother, cut up into small pieces. A photograph had been included inside the plastic bag. It was a picture of his mother kneeling in front of two men who had their knives raised over her. The day Azzam opened the "package" is the day he embraced the Ultimate Answer, committing his life to Jesus Christ as his Lord and Savior.

This is where the story gets even more incredible. Azzam sought out the two men who had butchered his mother and told them that he forgave them. He told them that Jesus loved them and that He could forgive murderers. The two men, Mahdi and Yasin, also claimed Jesus as their Savior. Then they confided to Azzam, "As we killed your mother, her last words were, 'Jesus, Jesus, I love You.'"

Without a doubt, Heaven has been and is being moved by these radical followers of Jesus. And while Somalia has yet to be changed, it will be. One heart at a time.[13]

CHAPTER 9

ANSWERED SPECIFICALLY

I know what it's like to pray generally and miss out on the blessing of receiving a specific answer. I also know what it's like to pray specifically.

God has answered many specific prayers for me, from small requests such as . . .

Locating an empty handicapped parking place
    when I took my husband to his doctor,
Finding the right gift for someone's birthday,
Bringing the dog back when he's run out of
    the yard,

Helping my granddaughter pull up her math grade.

To larger requests such as . . .

Meeting the deadline for submitting this
    manuscript,
Breaking open a passage of Scripture so that I have
    the framework for a message,
Giving me wisdom to answer media questions so
    that people are drawn to Jesus,
Enabling me to remain alert as I stayed with
    my mother all night before she moved to our
    Father's House.

To much greater requests such as . . .

Quickening someone's heart to embrace Jesus as
    Savior and Lord,
Healing my husband of the MRSA infection in his
    dialysis fistula,
Freeing me from anger and bitterness as I chose to
    forgive those who wounded me,
Bringing just the right people—my "generals"—to
    come alongside me and work at my ministry
    office . . .

I shared with you about the immediate answer
to prayer God gave me through His messenger, Ray

Bentley. On the Monday after Ray had encouraged me with the promise of generals, I joined my staff for prayer. We start our week together in worship and praise, and I shared Ray's words to me. Then I asked them to pray with me for the generals. Specifically, we asked God to bring additional personnel for each area that was lacking. And we asked Him to bring the generals to us. I, for one, did not want to have to go through public advertising or lengthy interview procedures.

One by one, over the space of the next six months, God brought us His choice for the staff positions. To be honest, it was a little slower than I would have liked. But I knew even then that God was testing my faith by stretching things out.

The first general God brought to us was something of a surprise, because he was a "he." Up until this point, our office had been staffed by women. But God was doing a new thing. The next was a single woman who helped coordinate our events. And then came a most remarkable young mother with an engineering degree who easily took over our IT. And then a director for our revivals who was the very best I could have imagined.

While I rejoiced over each person, I knew the most important position of all had yet to be filled: the operations manager. We needed someone who could oversee all the bits and pieces of the ministry while keeping everything on track and everyone working well together. And so I prayed. And prayed. And fasted. And prayed some more.

The board and I interviewed at least four people. We all agreed none of them seemed to be the general we were looking for. And then a résumé came to me in one of those encounters that seemed so casual as to be irrelevant. But when I read through the résumé, something seemed to click.

I set up a time to meet with this man one-on-one and go through the now-familiar questions of the interview. Because this person would interact not only with every staff member, but with the board and me, I felt I could not risk making a mistake. So I did something I almost never do. I laid out a "fleece." I did not lack faith. Instead, I was—like Gideon—seeking clear confirmation for God's perfect will in the course of action I would take because it involved the well-being of so many people, and the well-being of my ministry as a whole.

A fleece should be something that's logical but not probable unless God brings it to pass. As I was praying before the first interview, I asked God to give me His idea for a fleece. The thought that came to my mind was this: I asked God to have the gentleman ask me what name he should call me.

In all the interviews I've conducted in the thirty years AnGeL Ministries has been in existence, no one has ever asked me what they should call me. Because the staff had always been made up of women, it seemed natural to be called by my first name. But with a man I thought it might be different.

When the time came for the interview, I saw an unfamiliar car pull into the parking lot. Assuming it was the prospective operations manager, I went to the door of the office to greet him. We shook hands warmly, then as I guided him into the lobby area, he looked over his shoulder and said, "What should I call you?"[1] I had to restrain myself from shouting, "You're hired!" But we had two more rounds of interviews to go.

One of my board members later called him to go over practical details that included salary and benefits. When she reported to me the salary figure she had told him, I realized I had told him a different one. So as I went into the second one-on-one interview with him, I decided to put out another fleece. I asked God, when the question of his salary came up, to have this candidate tell me the figure didn't matter. I knew that was highly improbable for a man who was married with two college-age sons. But I was so afraid of making a mistake, and so desperate for God's perfect choice, and so aware that I could react emotionally to the relief of having someone for this position, that I just had to be sure.

When the subject of his salary came up in our second interview, I told this man that I had stated one figure and my board member had stated another. While I apologized for the confusion, I asked him for his thoughts. He responded by saying, "Miss Anne, it doesn't make any difference. Whatever you offer is fine." My second fleece was answered!

The third test I put this patient gentleman through was for him to sit down with all the staff for an interview. Their questions were specific. Some were tough, some were personal, all were used of God to penetrate below the surface and reveal the type of person he is. When he shared the testimony of his conversion, he wept. And we all wept with him as our hearts embraced the humble servant-leader God had brought to us as our last general. And we all hired him.

If I hadn't known it before, I knew it then with certainty: God answers specific prayers specifically. When we ask God for what He wants to give us, we can be sure He has a plan already in place. Our specific prayer gives us the thrill of not only participating in what He is doing, but knowing that we are part of a Divine plan.

One hundred years before Daniel prayed his prayer, God had put in place a plan that was revealed by Isaiah the prophet regarding Cyrus: "He is my shepherd and will accomplish all that I please; he will say of Jerusalem, 'Let it be rebuilt,' and of the temple, 'Let its foundations be laid.'"[2]

Keep in mind that Isaiah wrote this prophecy before the Babylonians invaded. Before the Jews were led off into captivity. Before Jerusalem was destroyed. Before the temple was looted and leveled. And if that wasn't dramatic enough, God had given to Isaiah further insight when He revealed,

> This is what the LORD says to his anointed, to Cyrus, whose right hand I take hold of to subdue nations before him . . . to open doors before him . . . : I will go before you. . . . I will give you hidden treasures . . . so that you may know that I am the LORD, the God of Israel, who summons you by name. For the sake of . . . Israel my chosen, I summon you by name and bestow on you a title of honor, though you do not acknowledge me. I am the LORD, and there is no other; apart from me there is no God. I will strengthen you . . . so that from the rising of the sun to the place of its setting people may know there is none besides me.[3]

In other words, God would do all of this, using Cyrus for the glory of His Name!

We are not told if Daniel knew of God's plan spoken through Isaiah. But he didn't need to know God's plan any more than you or I need to know it. God's promises are enough on which to base our prayers.

Three years after Daniel prayed, a new king took the throne in Persia. His name? Cyrus! And what was one of his first proclamations as king?

The LORD, the God of heaven, has given me all the kingdoms of the earth and he has appointed me to build a temple for him at Jerusalem in Judah. Anyone of his people among you— may his God be with him, and let him go up to Jerusalem in Judah and build the temple of the LORD, the God of Israel, the God who is in Jerusalem.[4]

There was no reason for the heart of Cyrus to be moved to let all God's people go home except that Daniel had prayed . . . and God had answered!

Not only did Cyrus tell the Jews that they could go home, but he gave them building materials for the temple. He gave them money. And he restored the temple vessels of gold and silver that had been looted by Nebuchadnezzar.[5]

So seventy years after their captivity had begun, a remnant of God's people under the leadership of Zerubbabel and Jeshua, arrived back home. And reality set in . . .

What must it have been like to climb the last of the Judean hills and look on the pile of rubble that had been the city of Jerusalem, the city of their God? How did they feel as they wandered through the burned-out houses and the broken-down buildings? Did tears flow freely as they picked their way through the ruins of what had been the temple?

To the eternal credit of the remnant's strength of resolve, they went to work, cleared the stones, and rebuilt the temple. When the temple was finished, the sound of weeping could be heard again. The old men were crying because to them, the rebuilt temple seemed "like nothing" compared to the glory of Solomon's original temple that they remembered.

God heard their cries and encouraged them by promising that He would "fill this house with glory . . . the glory of this present house will be greater than the glory of the former house."[6] Although the remnant had no way of knowing at the time, the house of God they rebuilt—and that King Herod later remodeled—would be the very place in which the baby Jesus was presented to God.[7] Twelve years after His presentation in the temple, it would be the place where the young boy Jesus sat "among the teachers, listening to them and asking them questions," amazing everyone with His understanding and His answers.[8] And when He began His public ministry, Jesus of Nazareth, the Lamb of God, the Messiah, the Redeemer of Israel, returned to walk in the same temple courts, to sit and teach on the same temple steps. And His presence "filled this house with glory."

I wonder . . . when the remnant who had returned from Persia offered the first sacrifice in the newly rebuilt temple, did they ever know that Daniel had prayed? I think not.

They didn't see in the shadows eight hundred miles east the figure of a man with a long gray beard. A man too old to make the trip to Jerusalem. A man looking out his open window, praying, pleading, pouring out his heart as he stood in the gap for his people. Holding God to His word as he prayed specifically.

But God knew. He saw and heard. And God's people were restored. Just as He promised.

PRAYER IS A BATTLE

At the end of this book, it's worth noting that when we pray like Daniel, we are entering into the realm of spiritual warfare with the enemy.

When it comes to our nation, we may think the real battle is with a political leader or corporate greed or the abortionists or radical terrorists or the school board or the city council. Yet the truth is that they are being manipulated by our adversary, the devil. Our real battle is not with a visible enemy at all. The real battle is "against the rulers, the authorities, the powers of this dark world, the spiritual forces of evil in the heavenly realms"—the invisible enemy who is manipulating the visible enemies like puppets to do his wicked will.

That's why I am firmly convinced that the primary answer to the mess our world finds itself in today is not politics. Or education. Or jobs. Or legislation. The primary, bottom-line answer is Daniel's God, who speaks to us through His Word and listens when we pray.

Not all prayers are answered immediately. And the waiting can be excruciating. But don't become discouraged when you lack evidence that your prayers are moving Heaven or changing anyone, much less a nation.

Six years after Daniel poured out his heart to God in urgent desperation for the nation of Judah,[1] he himself went through an agonizing delay. He had been given "a revelation." He knew that the revelation was true, and that it involved game-changing world events (10:1–2). But he couldn't comprehend what it meant.

During three weeks of Heaven's silence, Daniel went into a form of spiritual depression, unable to eat or even to bathe himself. It was as though his very life depended on a deeper understanding of God's Word. And then, after a delay of twenty-one days, the silence was broken. An answer was given through God's special messenger.

When the messenger addressed Daniel, twice in his response he described him as "you who are highly esteemed" (10:11, 19). Did Daniel think because this prayer had not been answered aws immediately as his previous prayer, that he had somehow fallen out of favor with God? That Heaven was no longer moved by his prayers?

Is that what you think? When God delays answering your prayer, do you think . . .

You're just not that important to Him?

You don't have enough faith?

You haven't used the right "formula" in prayer?

You haven't humbled yourself enough?

You haven't claimed just the right combination of His promises?

You haven't prayed long enough . . . or fervently enough . . . or specifically enough . . . or piously enough?

I've had some of those same thoughts when answers to my prayers have been delayed. But do you know something? Ninety-nine percent of the time, those thoughts are the hiss of the old serpent, the devil himself, slithering up and sowing suggestions in my ear, trying to undermine my confidence in God. The above list of thoughts are sneaky, subtle lies straight from the father of lies. So I just call him out. I rebuke him with the authority I have been given as a child of God. I claim the blood of Jesus to cover me and shield me from his vicious insinuations and accusations. Then I command him to leave as I keep on praying.

From the messenger's response and tone, it would seem that Daniel was feeling defeated by the unanswered prayer. Because the messenger immediately reassured Daniel, "Since the first day that you set your mind to gain understanding and to humble yourself before your God, your words were heard, and I have come in response to them" (10:12).

Could it be that God also wants to reassure you . . . *From the first day you set your mind to gain understanding through reading this book, and to humble yourself before your God by standing in the gap for your loved ones, your church, your nation, and your world, your words were heard. Heaven has been moved, and the promises of God are being fulfilled, one person at a time.*

You may not see the answer yet, but it is coming. Don't give up the fight!

Paul warns us that "we do not wage war as the world does. The weapons we fight with are not the weapons of the world. On the contrary, they have divine power to demolish strongholds."[2] Our primary offensive weapons are the Word of God, which is the Sword of the Spirit, and prayer. If you and I want to win the battle against the invisible enemy, we must pick up our Sword as we drop to our knees.

When we drop to our knees, the battle begins in earnest. The enemy will make you feel foolish for thinking you could take God at His Word. He will try to prevent you from prayer by convincing you are not a prayer warrior like so and so. That the prayers of one person won't really make any difference. Watch out! Can you see what's behind those tactics?

The messenger who came to Daniel after the twenty-one-day delay lifted the veil of invisibility that the enemy hides behind when he gave the reason for the delay: "The prince of the Persian kingdom resisted me twenty-one days. Then Michael, one of the chief princes, came to help me, because I was detained there with the king of Persia. Now I have come to explain to you what will happen to your people in the future . . ." (10:13–14).

While I don't understand all that the messenger said, I do know, and am convinced, that when we pray, we are entering into an invisible, spiritual realm where things are going on that we will never know about until we get to Heaven. That's one primary reason prayer is not easy. Prayer is the front line of the battle.

But be encouraged. Not only did Heaven respond to Daniel's cry, but Heaven rallied to Daniel's cause: another mighty messenger, Michael, came to help in the invisible battle and to ensure that Daniel's answer to prayer got through the fog of war.

When you and I pray, Heaven will respond and rally to our cause, whether we see visible evidence of it or not. Jesus Himself promised, "You may ask me for anything in my name, and I will do it."[3] Jesus also warned His followers that "in this world you will have trouble. But take heart! I have overcome the world."[4]

Because He has overcome, you and I will overcome also. At the end of human history as we know it, when the world seems totally dominated by the devil himself, the followers of Jesus will overcome the enemy "by the blood of the Lamb and by the word of their testimony."[5] King David, who was a mighty warrior, revealed the secret of his victories when he exclaimed, "Through God we will do valiantly, for *it is He* who shall tread down our enemies."[6]

That the "battle is the Lord's"[7] seems underscored by the fact that Daniel, battling in prayer, did so with "no strength left," "helpless," in "a deep sleep, with . . . face to the ground," "trembling," "speechless," "overcome with anguish."[8] Yet Daniel was victorious!

So remember this is war! But be encouraged!

One day, the enemy will be defeated. Finally. Completely. Eternally.

One day the golden bowls will be full of incense— the incense of our prayers gathered before the throne of God that trigger the biggest comeback of all time when Jesus returns to rule the world.[9]

One day you and I will join with millions upon millions of angels and other followers of Jesus, singing, "Worthy is the Lamb who was slain, to receive power and wealth and wisdom and strength and honor and glory and praise."[10]

One day the entire universe will rock in a victory chant of praise to the Lamb who has won the victory over all His enemies.

One day . . . on that day . . . we are going to say
every moment we spent in prayer that God used
to achieve victory for the glory of His Name was
worth it! *Praise God!*

Until that day, keep storming the gates of Heaven
with the promises of God.
For the glory of His Name!
Amen.

NOTES

INTRODUCTION

1. 2 Kings 17:16–23.
2. While there may have been others praying for God to fulfill His promise and return the captives to Judah, Daniel's prayer is the only one recorded in Scripture. I believe it is included in the biblical record to teach us not only how to pray for our people and our nation, but to underscore that the prayer of one person can move heaven and change a nation. Ezekiel 22:30.

CHAPTER 1

1. 1 Thessalonians 5:17.
2. My husband went to Heaven on August 19, 2015. It's interesting that after forty-nine years

of marriage, my commitment to him remains strong—even though he's gone.

3. Daniel 6:10.

4. Exodus 33:7–11.

5. Please visit my website, www.annegrahamlotz.org, and download our ministry app that offers free Bible study materials and devotionals. You can also sign up for our free e-devotional that will come to your inbox every day. It has a Scripture verse and brief application of what it means for life today.

6. Daniel 6:10.

7. Psalm 5:3; 88:13; 143:8.

8. Mark 1:35.

9. Revelation 3:1–3.

10. Psalm 94:14.

11. Romans 8:28.

12. www.gty.org/library/bibleqnas-library/QA0251 /how-did-the-magi-know-about-jesus.

Chapter 2

1. All references to the book of Daniel will be included in the text by chapter and verse.

2. Psalm 46:1–2.

3. Philippians 1:6.

4. 2 Timothy 4:6–8.

5. Reprinted as Anne Graham Lotz, *Daily Light Devotional* (Nashville: J. Countryman, a division

of Thomas Nelson, 1998). The foreword of this daily devotional will explain what a meaningful tool this has been in my family as the Truth has been passed down from generation to generation.

6. Haggai 2:4; Ephesians 6:10; Zechariah 8:9; Judges 6:14; 2 Corinthians 4:1; Galatians 6:9 all in the NKJV.

7. Visit my website, www.annegrahamlotz.org, click on *Studies in God's Word*, and then click on *Learning to Hear His Voice*. It's a free resource that will lead you through the steps of how to listen to God's voice. Or use this link to go directly: www.annegrahamlotz.org/learningtohearhisvoice/.

8. Genesis 6–8.

9. Genesis 18:16–19:29.

10. Miss Johnson's prayers were instrumental in establishing her international ministry, Bible Study Fellowship, that has brought millions of people into God's Word over the years it has been offered. Mother's prayers were instrumental in my father's ministry as he presented the Gospel face-to-face to over 200 million people in his lifetime, which changed many nations.

CHAPTER 3

1. Matthew 6:6.

2. Luke 5:16.

3. Luke 9:2–8. The story of the transfiguration is found in the Gospels of Matthew, Mark, and Luke.
4. This quote is taken from Mark 9:29 NKJV.
5. Matthew 6:16.
6. 1 Samuel 1.
7. 1 Samuel 2:26.
8. Luke 18:9.
9. The parable is found in Luke 18:9–14.
10. Proverbs 16:5.
11. Isaiah 66:2.
12. Daniel 2:48.

CHAPTER 4

1. James 2:17.
2. This prayer is based on the following verses: Matthew 24:35; Romans 3:23; 1 John 1:8–10; Acts 3:19; Ephesians 1:7–8; John 6:49–51; John 3:14–18; 1:16; 17:2–3.
3. John 10:28–30.
4. Hebrews 11:6.
5. Lamentations 3:19–23.
6. Job 2:9.
7. Genesis 3:5.
8. The story of the Exodus can be found in the Old Testament book by that name, chapters 1–14.
9. Exodus 14:31.

CHAPTER 5

1. Charles G. Finney, *How to Experience Revival* (New Kensington, Penn.: Whitaker House, 1984).

2. The most famous lighthouse in North Carolina is located on Hatteras Island and named, appropriately, the Cape Hatteras Lighthouse. Standing 210 feet tall, this black-and-white striped sentinel warns ships of its dangerous locale, an area of the Atlantic called Diamond Shoals, where the Gulf Stream collides with a colder current, creating optimal conditions for stormy seas, giant swells, and shifting sandbars. Over time, the beacon of light from the lighthouse has not grown dim. Instead, at various stages in its history, the power, clarity, number of reflectors, and visibility of the light have been increased. Today, it is clearly visible for twenty miles. And the light has never been allowed to go out. Even during the Civil War it was protected because of its strategic importance to the safety and well-being of the passing ships.

CHAPTER 6

1. For a more detailed account, please see Anne Graham Lotz, *Just Give Me Jesus* (Nashville: Nelson, 2000), 44–62.

2. John 2:3.
3. 2 Chronicles 7:15–16.
4. Genesis 18:16, 20–21.
5. Romans 8:27.
6. Genesis 19:15–16, 27–29.
7. John 14:26, 16:12.
8. One of the resources I keep in my place of prayer is a small volume that contains Scripture compilations for both morning and evening, 366 days of the year. The Holy Spirit has used this book more than any other book outside of my completed Bible to speak to me, giving insight and understanding as I pray: *Daily Light with Anne Graham Lotz* (Nashville: Countryman/Nelson, Nashville, 1998).

CHAPTER 7

1. 1 Kings 18.
2. Genesis 32:22–32.
3. 2 Timothy 3:16–17.

CHAPTER 8

1. Daniel 5.
2. Daniel was taken into captivity by Nebuchadnezzar in the first deportation in 605 BC. Jerusalem and the temple were destroyed by the Babylonians in 586 BC, approximately twenty years after Daniel's capture.

3. Ephesians 2:19–22; Hebrews 8:5.

4. John 3:16; Hebrews 10:5–10.

5. Revelation 21:1–3; 22:1–5.

6. 1 Timothy 2:3–6.

7. John 14:6.

8. 1 Timothy 1:15–16.

9. Acts 17:1–6.

10. Isaiah 6:8.

11. Fred Barlow, "William Carey: Missionary-Evangelist," *Wholesome Words* (1976), www.wholesomewords.org/missions/bcarey1.html.

12. Stephen Ross, "Charles Thomas (C.T.) Studd," *Wholesome Words* (2015), www.wholesomewords.org/missions/biostudd.html.

13. Tom Doyle, *Killing Christians* (Nashville: W Publishing Group, 2015), 1–17.

CHAPTER 9

1. For those who are curious, my answer was, "Miss Anne. All the men in the office call me that." (And of course, at the time we only had one other man in the office, but that's what he called me so that's what I said.)

2. Isaiah 44:28.

3. Isaiah 45:1–6.

4. Ezra 1:2–3.

5. Ezra 3:7; 5:14.

6. Haggai 2:7, 9.

7. Luke 2:22–24.
8. Luke 2:41–50.

Epilogue

1. He began the Daniel Prayer in the sixty-seventh year of captivity and the first year of the reign of Darius (implying he reigned for at least two years [Dan. 9:1]). The seventieth year, in the first year of the reign of Cyrus, the captives were set free (Ezra 1:1). The prayer he speaks of in Daniel 10 is uttered in the third year of Cyrus, making it approximately six years after Daniel 9.
2. 2 Corinthians 10:3–4.
3. John 14:14.
4. John 16:33.
5. Revelation 12:11.
6. Psalm 108:13 NKJV.
7. 1 Samuel 17:47.
8. Daniel 10:8–9, 11, 15–16.
9. Revelation 5:8.
10. Revelation 5:12–13.